MW01121447

ANOTHER COUNTRY

bloom

Guillermo Verdecchia

Talonbooks
Vancouver

Copyright © 2007 Guillermo Verdecchia

Talonbooks
P.O. Box 2076, Vancouver, British Columbia, Canada V6B 3S3
www.talonbooks.com

Typeset in Bembo and printed and bound in Canada.

First Printing: 2007

The publisher gratefully acknowledges the financial support of the Canada Council for the Arts; the Government of Canada through the Book Publishing Industry Development Program; and the Province of British Columbia through the British Columbia Arts Council and the Book Publishing Tax Credit for our publishing activities.

Library and Archives Canada Cataloguing in Publication

Verdecchia, Guillermo
    Another country ; Bloom / Guillermo Verdecchia ; introduction by Bruce Barton.

Plays.
ISBN 978-0-88922-570-1

    I. Verdecchia, Guillermo Bloom. II. Title.

PS8593.E67A76 2007   C813'.6   C2007-901059-8

CONTENTS

PREFACE

Two Plays about War

Another Country (originally *Final Decisions [WAR]*) was part of my response to Argentina's Dirty War (1976–83), during which the state security apparatus and its paramilitary assistants disappeared approximately 30,000 people as well as subjected them and others to routine torture. Still more were driven into exile. The period is well documented, and I won't describe or explain it too much here except to point out that the leaders of Argentina's military junta held that their campaign against leftist subversives and terrorists— or as one of them put it, against the children of Evita and Marx— was the beginning of the third world war. They called their comprehensive battle for hearts and minds the Process of National Reorganization, an effort that found ideological and material support in other Latin American countries and with powerful elements of the U.S. administration.

The aim of the Process was, according to the junta's leader, a transformation of the national consciousness. He explained that "a terrorist is not just someone with a gun or a bomb, but also someone who spreads ideas that are contrary to Western and Christian civilization."[1] Working with this helpful definition, the security apparatus disposed of urban guerrillas, union leaders, journalists, psychologists, Jews, students, and anyone else whose ideas might possibly, seemed to, or actually did, run counter to the

---

1. J. Patrice McSherry, *Predatory States: Operation Condor and Covert War in Latin America* (Lanham: Rowman & Littlefield, 2005), 1.

junta's understanding of Western and Christian civilization. The scale of the undertaking was defined by (yet) another general (probably trained in counter-insurgency at the U.S.-based and funded School of the Americas, or the School of the Coups as it's known in Latin America), who announced, "First we will kill all the subversives; then, their collaborators; later, those who sympathize with them; afterward, those who remain indifferent; and finally, those who are undecided."[2] The public relations firm Burson-Marsteller was hired to make Argentina look good while the junta and its collaborators reorganized the nation.

bloom began as an attempt to adapt T. S. Eliot's poem, *The Waste Land,* for the stage. It seemed to me an ideal project to undertake with Soheil Parsa, whom I have long considered to be one of the finest directors in Canada. When Eliot's estate refused permission for the adaptation, I decided to take some of the material we had generated while working with a group of actors and try to come up with a play inspired by the ideas that had appealed to us in *The Waste Land.* The poem fairly overflowed with images (sighing crowds "undone" by death in the "unreal city," and "hooded hordes swarming over endless plains, stumbling in cracked earth," among others) that seemed contemporaneous in the context of the destruction of Afghanistan and Iraq (all part of the larger effort of international reorganization we know as the War on Terror). For me, *bloom* quickly became, in part, a (more or less) imaginative exploration of a world perpetually at war.

I find interesting continuities and correspondences between these two plays, my first full-length drama and my latest, and I hope these sympathies and continuities will be of interest to some readers. I hope most of all that these texts might continue to serve as blueprints for productions.

Guillermo Verdecchia, Toronto 2007

2. Tom H. Hastings, *Nonviolent Response to Terrorism* (North Carolina: McFarland, 2004), 14.

INTRODUCTION

I called boldly, "Stand and unfold yourself."

—Gerontion, *bloom*

Describing *Another Country* and *bloom* as two plays about war may initially appear a bit like using the term "Impala" to correlate a breed of African antelope and a specific model of Chevrolet automobile. That is, it is the differences between them that are most conspicuous. *Another Country* is, fittingly, a youthful play, robust with attitude and energy, testing the seams of its adopted conventions and straining the confines of its own sharp, critical intelligence. Marked by short scenes, precisely etched characterization, and abrupt shifts into graphic materiality, this early work both emulates and dissects contemporaneous stylistics of the late 1980s and early 1990s. In the process, it performs both its engagement with and its resistance to its original contexts (aesthetic, political, commercial, personal). *bloom*, by contrast, is a conspicuously mature piece of writing, delightfully uncharacteristic in its consistent restraint and anachronistic in its reliance on metaphor and lyricism. Reflective, poetic, allusive, *bloom* is an alarmingly patient play, its calm progression a source of gradual, inevitable tension, unease, self-consciousness, and, potentially, revelation.

However (leaving behind the antelope/automobile analogy), the two plays demonstrate their shared authorship in key manners (both polite and otherwise). In fact, *Another Country* exhibits many of Verdecchia's enduring strategies, and it is both intriguing and instructive to trace them through to his most recent work in *bloom*. In both its original title—*Final Decisions (WAR)*—and its current one, *Another Country* activates Verdecchia's trademark integration of anger and/of/about/towards/despite ambivalence. The parallels established between advertising and marketing on the one hand and oppression and torture on the other are provocative in both their oversimplification and their precise distillation, successfully rendering state and individual brutality with both critical detachment *and* irrational immediacy. As in virtually all of Verdecchia's subsequent plays—indeed, all his subsequent writing across genres and media— *Another Country* manages to portray both the striking clarity of isolated situations, events, and decisions and the equally striking complexity of the contexts in which they occur and evolve. The result confounds simple oppositions of naïveté and sophistication, activism and pacifism, guilt and innocence, as both the playwright and his audience are enfolded within a shared yet critical *act* of complicity.

It is thus not difficult to recognize in *Another Country* the roots of later plays such as *Fronteras Americanas* (1993), *A Line in the Sand* (1995, with Marcus Youssef), and even *The Adventures of Ali & Ali and the Axes of Evil* (2004, with Youssef and Camyar Chai). Each of these works shares with this early play an overt engagement with politics, made manifest in large part through distinctly performative strategies. By contrast, the connection between *Another Country* and *bloom* is less direct and distinct. In the latter play, the aged, near-blind Gerontion confidently asserts: "Remembering is overrated. Won't solve anything. Believe me." This effort towards willed forgetfulness (distantly yet unmistakably resonant of the deeply troubled social conscience of the Argentina portrayed in *Another Country*) pervades much of the play. Resigned self-deceit is tentatively proposed as the sole effective survival tactic in a (remarkably familiar) world gone mad. The play's connections to history are tenuous and mutable, anchored in poetic, philosophical, and journalistic word patternings, the arrangements and meanings of which are uniformly abstract and subjective. The telescopic, period-specific intensity of *Another Country* is, in *bloom*, inverted and exploded; despite its topicality, in the later play the audience sits within the eerie, shadow-filled silence of a descending mushroom cloud, as if after the end of endings. Little surprise, then, that *bloom* embodies its lineage in Beckett and Eliot's *The Wasteland* more conspicuously than in the urgency of Verdecchia's previous efforts.

Ultimately, however, *bloom*, in its philosophical, even mythological reach, is about potential and rejuvenation. It is, therefore, also about struggle and resistance. Although the assessment that "People don't move on. We're still living in caves" is given multiple expressions throughout its pages, it is the Boy's "I want more. There's more" that rings clearest and most resonant. *bloom* is also about poetry—that which is lost and lamented and disfigured by the impersonal brutality of quotidian reality, performed nationalisms, and the complicity of apathetic indifference. But it is also about the poetry that emerges, raw, ragged, and ravenous, from beneath the ashes. In a sense, *bloom* is about the poetry of resistance—perhaps even the *poetics* of resistance. And I know of few poetics that are not thoroughly informed by both anger and ambivalence. It is possible, then, to see *Another Country* and *bloom* as bookends on a set of ideas and preoccupations, but also, and perhaps even more so, on a set of vigorously *enacted* principles and beliefs.

When, late in *bloom*, the Boy asks, "Is this true? Is this the story?", he voices the playwright's perpetual insistence that "truth" and "stories" be engaged in the same breath, the same moment, the same argument, the same world. To stand, thus, and unfold oneself is, of course, an extremely naïve and extremely sophisticated act—which also makes it one of extreme courage. And this, at the risk of my own provocative oversimplification, is the demand of both of these plays, as it is that of the full body of Guillermo Verdecchia's dramatic *oeuvre*.

Bruce Barton

Another Country

Another Country was first produced as *Final Decisions* at Alberta Theatre Projects PlayRites in 1991 with the following cast and crew:

BEATRICE .... Janet Lo
MONICA .... Shawna-Lori Burnett
MARIE .... Loretta Bailey
TONY .... Eric Trask
MARK .... Christopher Hunt

Director: Sharon Pollock
Sound design: Allan Rae
Set design: Terry Gunvordahl
Costume design: John Pennoyer
Lighting design: Harry Frehner

It was subsequently produced at Station Street Theatre in Vancouver under the direction of Paul Crepeau with the following cast:

BEATRICE .... Tamsin Kelsey
MONICA .... Jennifer Griffin
MARIE .... Leslie Ewen
TONY .... Guillermo Verdecchia
MARK .... Sam Malkin

For M.S.A.

Scene 1

Upscale restaurant.

BEATRICE:
I'm going to turn that place around. I can't believe some of the garbage that people get away with—unimaginative, boring. They're putting out the same stuff they did in school. Not anymore.

TONY:
Look out.

BEATRICE:
They better look out. It's great to finally have some real responsibility.

TONY:
You mean power.

BEATRICE:
Sure power. But I want to use it responsibly. I can really make some changes.

TONY:
Mark said the same thing to me the other day. I'll have more latitiude now. Won't have to go running for permission if I want to do something out of the ordinary.

BEATRICE:
Exactly. We don't have to explain every little thing. I have the authority to make sure things are done right.

TONY:
You mean your way.

BEATRICE:

Of course. My way is the right way.

TONY:

Oh I know it.

BEATRICE:

There's no excuse for some of the appalling work the agency's put out. We have a responsibility. To our clients, to the consumer and to the industry itself.

TONY:

Of course.

BEATRICE:

I'm sorry, I've been talking non-stop.

TONY:

It's all right. You're excited about it.

BEATRICE:

I am. Do you know I'm the youngest person to make VP? Not to mention the only woman.

TONY:

How do you know?

BEATRICE:

I looked it up.

TONY:

I love you.

BEATRICE:

I love you too.

They kiss.

TONY:

You know, I was thinking we should start looking for that new house. On the Hill.

BEATRICE:

Really?

TONY:
Absolutely. It's not as if we can't afford it.

BEATRICE:
I can't believe our luck.

TONY:
What luck?

BEATRICE:
Everything working out so perfectly. Your promotion, now mine ...

TONY:
That's not luck, that's hard work. We deserve it.

Shift in lights. BEATRICE and TONY at dinner / BEATRICE and MONICA at office.

BEATRICE:
Have a seat Monica.

MONICA:
Thank you.

BEATRICE:
I understand you have some objections to the ad for Major Electronix.

MONICA:
Yes. I do.

TONY:
What's the image?

BEATRICE:
There's a very clean, sleek metal table. Italian. On the table there's a CD player or DVD player completely disassembled. Pieces very carefully arranged on the table. Overhead, a single bare light bulb—no shade—just a bare bulb hanging from a wire right?

TONY:
Uh huh.

17

BEATRICE:

Behind the table there's a guy in a long trench coat—or a doctor's gown—I don't know yet. So this guy's got a clipboard in his hand oh and mirrored shades reflecting the pieces on the table—clipboard, right. And you can make out a form on the clipboard that says "Confession" in big letters at the top—or maybe "Quality Confession", something like that, and the tag at the bottom says "We have ways of making them talk." What do you think?

TONY:

Well, it ...

BEATRICE:

Tell me. Tell me about your objections. Right now, face to face. I'd like to hear it from you. Not third-hand. The floor is yours. I'm listening. (*Pause.*) What's wrong? Would it be easier for you if I turned my back?

MONICA:

I don't think you're—

BEATRICE:

What's that? I can't hear you. Speak up.

TONY:

It's good, but it sounds a little ...

BEATRICE:

You don't like it. You have to picture it: very smooth, very sexy—the pieces all carefully arranged, maybe a pair of tweezers, the guy with the mirrored shades, maybe a couple of muscle guys in the background ... It's funny. Jesus, I mean quality control for electronics is not the most exciting thing to work with.

TONY:

I like it. I think it's good.

MONICA:

I said I don't think you're really interested in my objections.

BEATRICE:
You don't think I'll be able to follow the elevated ethical argument? You're right actually. I don't understand your argument but not because it's too sophisticated. No, I can't understand your objections because I can't understand censorship. That's what it comes down to doesn't it? You think it's "offensive" so it shouldn't be printed. I never noticed censor on your job description.

I'm shocked Monica. I'm shocked, first because you find the ad "totally offensive." Isn't that what you said? Never mind where I heard. And I'm shocked that you didn't have the nerve to discuss your feelings with me. I took a big chance hiring you but I hired you because I thought you were bright and imaginative. Turns out I was wrong. Don't you have a sense of humour?

TONY:
I like it.

BEATRICE:
Do you? Do you think it's funny?

TONY:
Sure.

MONICA:
There is nothing funny about that ad.

BEATRICE:
I guess you don't have a sense of humour.

MONICA:
My sense of humour is not the issue.

BEATRICE:
What is the issue?

MONICA:
Torture.

TONY:
I think it's great.

BEATRICE:
That ad has nothing to do with torture. It refers to B–movies. It's a joke. Why you would object to it is beyond me. Although, it is in keeping with your work lately: a lot of noise but no results. I'm sure you're aware that your performance lately has been less than acceptable.

MONICA:
Yes I'm aware of that.

BEATRICE:
Is there any reason you can offer to explain why?

MONICA:
I'm … no, there's no reason.

BEATRICE:
Is there any reason why we should keep you on here? I get the impression that you're not very interested in staying with the firm.

MONICA:
Not really.

BEATRICE:
Is it something personal? With your boyfriend perhaps?

MONICA:
That's none of your business.

BEATRICE:
It is if it affects your work.

MONICA:
I quit.

BEATRICE:
I fired her.

TONY:
Because she didn't like your ad?

BEATRICE:
No, her work was terrible. It's a shame, I liked her. Remember Monica? I told you about her.

TONY:
Can't say that I do.

BEATRICE:
Doesn't matter. She doesn't work for us anymore.

TONY:
Doesn't work for you.

BEATRICE:
It's not my company.

TONY:
Not yet.

BEATRICE:
No, not yet.

Scene 2

Morning.

MARIA:
Did you bring coffee?

MONICA:
Yes. Cost me a small fortune but I got it. Do you want some now?

MARIA:
No. Let's wait. Let's delay our gratification till we're desperate for it. Context is everything.

MONICA:
You're nuts.

MARIA:
Yes, yes I am. I'm glad you came over.

An awkward hug.

MONICA:
Because I brought coffee?

MARIA:
Not just the coffee. I'll bet you brought cigarettes too.

MONICA:
Since when do you smoke?

MARIA:
I don't smoke out of context but in this context I feel like having one.

MONICA:
I quit.

MARIA:
You quit.

MONICA:
Months ago.

MARIA:
Hey, did you notice if the phone on the corner was working?

MONICA:
No.

MARIA:
It's not working?

MONICA:
I didn't notice.

MARIA:
So … How's Lucinda?

MONICA:
Lucinda's gone.

MARIA:
Gone?

MONICA:
They grabbed her leaving the restaurant three days ago. I locked myself in. Today's the first day I left the apartment.

MARIA:
(*lying*) It's all right. You're safe here.

Scene 3

At work.

MARK:
Have you got the master?

TONY:
Yes. Have you got the video?

MARK:
Where's the updates for the upstairs file?

TONY:
Updates for upstairs. I don't know. I gave them to you.

MARK:
Well I don't have them. I've got every other team's updates
here. Where the fuck?

TONY:
Relax, it'll turn up. It's gotta be here somewhere.

MARK:
Relax he says. Relax. If I'd known you were such a
disorganized slacker I'd never have recommended you.

TONY:
I'm disorganized? You had the updates.

MARK:
I categorically deny any knowledge of ever having—and you
didn't sign this.

TONY:
Didn't sign what?

MARK:
Transfers. And look, this is incomplete.

He shows TONY the form.

TONY:
Just make something up.

MARK:

We can't do that.

TONY:

Oh come on. They're transfers—what are we going to do, go back into the files? We'll be here till Christmas. Just make something up. Who'll know?

He scribbles something on the sheet.

Anything else?

MARK:

No, we're done except for the update.

TONY:

I'll take care of it in the morning. I'll put another one together.

MARK:

You know there're more coming in right away.

TONY:

More?

MARK:

The hotel's gonna be full up.

TONY:

When?

MARK:

The next—

TONY:

Week?

MARK:

Forty-eight hours.

TONY:

Where do they come from?

MARK:

They're shit you scrape off your shoes.

Scene 4

Late night.

MONICA:
So now I've got all the testimonies. 146 pages. Personal accounts, descriptions, names. 146 pages of pain.

MARIA:
What are you going to do with them?

MONICA:
Lucinda was—is—Lucinda is connected to a group, like Amnesty. The idea was to get this out of the country to them.

MARIA:
Let the world know?

MONICA:
To create some kind of international pressure.

MARIA:
Political pressure? Do you think anyone with any power cares?

MONICA:
People don't know what's going on here.

MARIA:
People don't care.

MONICA:
They don't know. I didn't.

MARIA:
I tried telling you about it a thousand times.

MONICA:
I didn't understand how bad it was until Lucinda got me working on this. It's ludicrous. A stack of papers. Some nights when we were working on this though … it felt like we were building a bomb. We were so nervous about it. We wouldn't type any later than eleven. We were so paranoid we thought the neighbours would hear us and figure out what we were

25

up to. It felt so dangerous. I used to practically have a heart attack every time I had to photocopy something. I used the copier at work. I was sure somebody would come by and see what I was up to.

Looks like a stack of scrap paper now. We must know someone who can do something with this.

MARIA:
You mean people from the paper?

MONICA:
Yeah.

MARIA:
When was the last time you saw any of them, Monica? They're gone.

MONICA:
There must be someone who—

MARIA:
Don't look at me. I don't do paperwork. I have no contacts that would be any good for this sort of thing. Maybe two years ago ... and everybody Mom or Dad knew left a long time ago. Left or ...

MONICA:
It was so hard. Sometimes I couldn't type I was crying so much. If I'd had a gun ... well, I can see how somebody might ...

MARIA:
I don't think there's a choice anymore. It's a matter of self-defence.

MONICA:
Violence will only lead to more violence.

MARIA:
Violence, eventually, has to be met with violence.

MONICA:
No it doesn't.

MARIA:

Oh, that's right, I forgot. You're the expert. You know all about this sort of thing. You're the one who never went to a demonstration because you knew instinctively that it was a waste of time. You're the one who wouldn't sign a petition because in your words, "It's better to work with the system." After what happened to Dad ... ?

MONICA:

I was too young.

MARIA:

You were twenty years old. You were a coward, you—

MONICA:

I don't want to go over this anymore.

MARIA:

I do.

How long have I been at this, Monica? How many protests, actions, letters—I've done the peaceful channels, the legitimate channels for five years now. Five years that you sat out and maybe you were right because what has it amounted to? Nothing. They laugh at us. Sure, march all over downtown once a week, makes the government look tolerant and nothing changes.

Five years, that you spent on the sidelines, shaking your head, while every other day I lost somebody else and now that you've had a big adventure typing up a pile of crap you want to tell me again what should and shouldn't be done?

MONICA:

I lost people too. (*Silence.*) Are you serious? Maria? About violence?

MARIA:

You sound like Mum. "Are you serious Maria?" "Maria, who put those ideas into your head?"

MONICA:

"What have you been reading?" (*Silence.*) Do you know what I found the other day? Old pictures of Mom and Dad in leather jackets looking so cool on the motorcycle.

The lights suddenly go out. A burst of gunfire from off.

MARIA:

Get down!

Two men enter, there is a short struggle. MARIA is knocked out.

MONICA:

Leave her alone.

She is knocked unconscious and dragged off.

Scene 5

Phone booth. MARIA phones a friend.

MARIA:

They took Monica. My sister Monica. Just now. At home. She was with me. No I'm fine. They think they've got me.

What am I going to do? No I'll come up. Wait for me at the bar.

Scene 6

BEATRICE and TONY—early evening.

BEATRICE:

Did you read this?

TONY:

What is it?

BEATRICE:

Story about a woman who killed her husband.

TONY:

Oh yeah.

BEATRICE:

They were married nineteen years and apparently he used to beat her all the time. He'd get drunk and beat her up. Broke her ribs, left her unconscious. She was afraid he'd kill her one day so she set fire to his bed while he was sleeping. The court let her go.

TONY:

They let her go?

BEATRICE:

Her lawyer claimed it was self-defence.

TONY:

Self-defence. What a pile of shit.

BEATRICE:

Well, she felt her life was threatened.

TONY:

Fine. She should have called the police.

BEATRICE:

The police never do anything about domestic violence.

TONY:

So you think she was justified?

BEATRICE:

No, but—

TONY:

You don't take the law into your own hands—

BEATRICE:

I don't know—20 years of abuse—

TONY:

There are systems set up to protect people and administer justice. I'm not saying she didn't have a valid case, but she broke the law. They never should have let her go.

BEATRICE:

Okay. Don't get excited. I'm not planning to burn you.

TONY:

How can I be sure? Now I won't be able to sleep.

BEATRICE:

I promise I won't burn you.

TONY:

Better not. 'Cause if you do, I'll have to get nasty.

BEATRICE:

Oh. How nasty?

TONY:

You're not too old to be spanked, young lady.

BEATRICE:

I'm sorry. I promise I'll never set fire to your bed again.

TONY:

That's better. Now come and give your old man a kiss.

They kiss.

Scene 7

Box 1. MARK, TONY, MONICA.

MONICA in a small square room. There should be nothing "mysterious" about this space. Flat, ugly lighting. MONICA kneels with her arms parallel to the floor (airplane position). After 30 seconds ...

TONY:

You can put your arms down now. Would you like a cigarette? Just nod your head if you do. You don't have to speak. You can massage your arms if you like. Would you like something to drink?

Scene 8

Coke break. MARK and TONY—office.

MARK:
You've never done coke. Really?

TONY:
Really. I've led a sheltered life.

MARK:
(*as TONY is about to snort*) Breathe in. Not out. And don't sneeze.

TONY:
Yeah, thanks. I know how to do it. I've seen it in movies.

MARK:
Shut up and snort.

TONY does. He wiggles his nose.

Do another.

TONY:
Yeah?

MARK:
Yeah. What do you think I'm going to give you one and do five myself?

TONY:
I don't know. This stuff's expensive.

MARK:
Shut up and honk.

TONY does one line.

Now one more up the other side for balance.

MARK snorts expertly, wiping excess coke with finger and rubbing it in his gums. TONY wiggles his nose and sniffles. MARK looks at him expectantly. TONY looks at MARK.

TONY:
I don't feel anything.

31

MARK:
    You will.

TONY:
    Does everybody down here do this?

MARK:
    Pretty much.

TONY:
    Frank?

MARK:
    Sure. Frank, Danny, Seba, Leo, Pockets, Don—

TONY:
    Leo?

MARK:
    Yeah, Leo. And Colin, and Eddie, and Norman. He's a fiend,
    Norman. Adam.

TONY:
    Little Adam, the, with the glasses? I don't believe it.

MARK:
    Believe it. Little Adam, all of them. And absolutely everybody
    in the Olympic wing.

TONY:
    Shit. What if Pinhead comes down?

MARK:
    Where do you think we get it?

TONY:
    He gave it to you?

MARK:
    A little bonus. Incentive. (*producing cigarettes*) Would you like a
    cigarette?

TONY:
    Sure. Huh. That's funny. You said that just like you do inside.

MARK:
Yeah?

They are high, sniffing, agitated, speedy.

TONY:
How many do we have to get through tonight?

MARK:
Two but I think we could do more.

TONY:
Yeah, I could do a bus load.

MARK:
You want some more?

TONY:
Sure.

MARK lines up more.

Sometimes I can't believe the stuff Pinhead wants from these people. Half of these shits don't know anything.

MARK:
Every one of them is here for a reason.

TONY:
Of course, of course. Such a drag for a handful of names.

MARK:
Every one of those names brings us one step closer *(snorts)* one step closer.

TONY:
Step closer to what? *(snorts)*

MARK:
One step closer to having everything under control. It's huge complicated. It's a very complex. They're everywhere. It involves ... It extends ... It's very involved and extended.

TONY:
I wonder ... Don't you think that sometimes ... it's hard sometimes. I find it hard sometimes.

33

MARK:

> You can't think like that. Have another.

> *TONY shakes his head no.*

> Have another. You can't ... As soon as you start to worry ... if you worry about whether or not it's right ... You do what you have to. Doubt ... if you start to doubt you're finished.

TONY:

> I don't have a problem ... Don't you ever ... ?

MARK:

> You have to be strong. We have to be so clear and sure. "In this world ye shall have tribulations but be of good cheer ... "

> Should we get to work?

Scene 9

> *The Box. MARK, TONY and MONICA.*

TONY:

> We want you to be comfortable. Don't you want anything to drink? I want to help you. I'm your friend. If you don't want to speak you can just indicate with your head yes or no, all right? Just nod your head. You don't have to say a word if you don't want to. Don't worry. I won't hurt you. I want to help you. I'm your friend.

> Just nod your head, all right?

Scene 10

> *BEATRICE and TONY. A restaurant.*

BEATRICE:

> You hardly touched your food. You've barely said two words all night. If there's something on your mind, I wish you'd—

TONY:

I'm tired okay? I work just as hard as you do, if not harder.

BEATRICE:

Is that what this is about? My work? You're what ... envious?

TONY:

Don't be stupid. I didn't say—

BEATRICE:

Don't call me stupid. How the hell do I know what you're talking about? I'm supposed to guess what you're thinking. You never tell me anything. You're miserable all the time lately ...

TONY:

Enough. Okay. Jesus, you should know better.

BEATRICE:

What does that mean?

TONY:

You're in marketing—if you want to get a point across, you don't shove it down somebody's throat, you put it across carefully.

BEATRICE:

I'm not talking about marketing. We're married, remember?

TONY:

I'm tired.

BEATRICE:

Why don't you take some time off? We could take a holiday.

TONY:

You love your job.

BEATRICE:

We're not talking about my job.

TONY:

Maybe I want to talk about your job.

BEATRICE:

Tony ...

TONY:

    I can't take time off work.

BEATRICE:

    Why not?

TONY:

    Because I can't.

BEATRICE:

    They won't give it to you or you don't want to?

TONY:

    You're really starting to piss me off.

BEATRICE:

    Well you're pissing me off.

TONY:

    They won't give me time off.

BEATRICE:

    Have you asked?

TONY:

    No.

BEATRICE:

    Do you want some time off?

TONY:

    They wouldn't let me have it.

BEATRICE:

    What the hell do you do that's so goddamned important you can't get time off?

TONY:

    Nothing.

BEATRICE:

    You haven't answered my question.

TONY:

    I'm not going to.

BEATRICE:

Why are you like this?

TONY:

Like what?

BEATRICE:

You're being an asshole.

TONY:

I am an asshole.

BEATRICE:

That's true but it's not good enough. Will you ask about some time off? Please, for me?

TONY:

They don't care that my wife is concerned about our relationship.

BEATRICE:

Do they care about you? That you're under a lot of stress?

TONY:

They care about getting the job done. Look, things are very tense right now. We've got a huge work load and we're understaffed.

BEATRICE:

And me? What am I supposed to do? When you're edgy all the time and working 17 hours a day and not talking to me and not making love and—

TONY:

Go out and get yourself a lover.

BEATRICE:

I just might.

TONY:

Fuck off Beatrice.

BEATRICE:

No you fuck off. (*Silence.*) I don't even know what you do at work.

TONY:
Come on.

BEATRICE:
I know you're head of Human Resource Management for the Political Section. I have no idea what that means.

TONY:
I monitor people involved in fringe or marginal political activities. I compile information. It's completely mundane. I'm a civil servant. I keep track of people and compile information. That's it.

BEATRICE:
Then I don't understand. Will you ask about some time off?

TONY:
What the hell good would time off be if you're going to keep harassing me with your stupid questions every 20 seconds?

Scene 11

BEATRICE answers the phone.

BEATRICE:
Hello. Hello?

MARIA:
Is Anthony there?

BEATRICE:
Tony? No, he's not in. Can I take a message?

MARIA:
He's not there?

BEATRICE:
No. Who is this?

MARIA:
Tell him Maria called.

BEATRICE:
Maria?

MARIA:
Yes.

BEATRICE:
Do you work with him?

MARIA:
Tell him I called.

BEATRICE:
Does he have your number?

MARIA:
Make sure he knows I called.

Scene 12

Bar.

TONY:
I'm just tired. I'm—I had a fight with Bea.

MARK:
Oh yeah.

TONY:
I'm having some problems—you know—uh, dealing with things.

MARK:
What things?

TONY:
Work. I'm not eating and I can't sleep.

MARK:
Stress.

TONY:
Yeah.

MARK:
What was the fight about?

TONY:

Bea says I never talk to her. She wants me to take some time off.

MARK:

What for?

TONY:

She thinks I'm burned out. Need a break.

MARK:

Do you feel burned out?

TONY:

Not really. A little tired maybe. When you and Diane—when you were married—did she know?

MARK:

No.

TONY:

How did you—did you ever have any problems?

MARK:

Yeah. I used to wake up screaming. You get over it. You just have to discipline yourself.

TONY:

You never told her anything?

MARK:

No. You can't Tony. They don't understand.

TONY:

But Bea is—

MARK:

Bea is a very smart lady but I doubt she could understand what it's all about.

TONY:

It seems sort of unfair.

MARK:

Not really. It would just cause her a lot of grief. Be patient. Tell her it's stress. She'll understand.

TONY:
Yeah.

MARK:
And if you ever want to talk about it, I'm always here. I know what it's like.

TONY:
Thanks.

MARK:
Hey don't thank me. I get paid for this.

Scene 13

MARIA phones TONY. BEATRICE listens.

TONY:
Hello.

MARIA:
This is Maria.

TONY:
Sorry?

MARIA:
The woman you have in the basement of the Naval School is my sister.

TONY:
Who is this?

MARIA:
I'm the one you want. Let her go. She's of no use to you.

TONY:
You have the wrong number.

MARIA:
I'll turn myself in. Let her go.

TONY:
I'm sorry, you've got the wrong—

MARIA:

I'll kill you.

TONY hangs up.

BEATRICE:

Who was that?

TONY:

Some lunatic. Wrong number.

BEATRICE:

Someone named Maria called for you.

TONY:

What?

BEATRICE:

I said someone named Maria called for you. Was that her now?

TONY:

When did she call?

BEATRICE:

Who is she?

TONY:

When did she call? Why didn't you tell me before?

BEATRICE:

She called yesterday.

TONY:

She's nobody you know.

BEATRICE:

How do you know her?

TONY:

She was brought in and detained.

BEATRICE:

How can she be calling if she's been detained?

TONY:

Obviously it's someone else claiming to be this woman.

BEATRICE:
Why would someone claim to be this woman?

TONY:
Bea, the less you know about this the better it is. If she calls again you let me know right away. Bea?

BEATRICE:
What is going on?

TONY:
This is no game Bea. Tell me if she calls again.

BEATRICE:
And if I don't?

TONY:
Then things might get difficult for us.

BEATRICE:
Who's us?

TONY:
Mark and me. And you too.

Scene 14

The Box. MARK, TONY and MONICA.

TONY:
Is that your name? Maria? That's the name we have here. Is it correct? Just nod your head. Yes or no. You don't have to speak. Please just answer the question. All you have to do is nod your head. You have to help me. I'm trying to help you.

Pause.

You're making this very difficult. You're making this much more difficult than it has to be.

Scene 15

MARK's visit. MARK chopping coke.

MARK:

I get it cheap from a friend. I don't pay the full price. It's amazing what some people will pay for it.

BEATRICE:

Whatever the market will bear.

She snorts.

MARK:

Exactly. If I had to pay full price I wouldn't buy it.

BEATRICE:

Sure.

MARK:

I wouldn't.

He snorts.

TONY:

Don't you worry about carrying it around?

MARK:

Why? I'll get arrested?

TONY:

Sure. They'll drag you into the Box and ....

BEATRICE:

What's the Box?

MARK:

That's what we call the room where we do our interviews. It's small and square.

TONY:

Like a box.

MARK:

Hence the name. It's a very sophisticated system we got down there.

TONY:
Very sophisticated.

MARK:
Smoke?

BEATRICE:
Thanks.

TONY:
Mmmn.

MARK lights all three cigarettes.

BEATRICE:
Ah, ah, don't light it.

MARK:
(*lighting his own*) Why not?

TONY:
Third light off a match. Bad luck.

MARK:
Why?

TONY:
It comes from the war.

BEATRICE:
The trenches.

TONY:
Because of the gas.

MARK:
You sure it's not like walking under a ladder?

TONY:
What?

MARK:
You don't walk under a ladder because it's bad luck.

BEATRICE:
It's exactly like that except there's a real reason for it.

MARK:

There's a real reason for not walking under a ladder too.

BEATRICE:

What?

MARK:

It's bad luck.

They laugh.

No, it's bad luck be—

TONY:

Oh, I remember. The enemy would see the first light, aim on the second and then shoot on the third ... or something.

BEATRICE:

It wasn't the gas?

TONY:

No. I just remembered. Sorry, tell us about the ladders.

MARK:

A ladder forms a triangle which stands for the Holy Trinity: Father, Son and Holy Ghost. Walking under a ladder defies the Trinity.

BEATRICE:

Not to mention the fact that something might fall on you.

MARK:

Should we do some more?

TONY:

I can see how it would be easy to get hooked on this stuff.

MARK:

Nobody with any will power gets hooked. Requires a little discipline that's all. This world, this life was meant to be enjoyed and I plan to enjoy it. And God saw that it was good ...

BEATRICE:

(*snorts*) You think God meant for us to do cocaine?

MARK:

Christ drank wine didn't he?

BEATRICE:
Not to get drunk.

MARK:
You don't think they were drunk at Cana? And anyway, I don't see you refusing to do coke.

BEATRICE:
I'm not complaining. I have no problems with coke. But I don't need to quote the Bible to justify my vices either.

MARK:
It's not a vice.

Silence.

TONY:
Mark's right: we're all good people and we work hard and let's enjoy it while we can.

BEATRICE:
You really do believe in God.

MARK:
You have to believe.

TONY:
I don't have to do anything.

MARK:
Look, there's an order right? Night day. Right wrong. Where does that order come from? From God. If there was no order the world would be a disaster.

BEATRICE:
It is.

MARK:
Your life is a disaster?

BEATRICE:
No my life isn't.

MARK:
And why is that?

BEATRICE:
Because I'm lucky.

MARK:
Luck has nothing to do with it. Your life is fine because you are a decent person. A good person.

TONY:
We're all basically good people.

BEATRICE:
The world is full of good people who suffer ...

MARK:
We don't suffer?

BEATRICE:
People who are persecuted ... who go hungry and—

MARK:
"Persecuted"? You talking about this country Bea? People who go hungry? You mean The Poor? Remember Bea, I was poor. I grew up in that shit and let me tell you, those people—the poor who suffer—most of them were lazy thieves. They deserved whatever they got. There is a reason for everything and those who go against the order—those who aren't upright—suffer for it.

You don't believe in God.

BEATRICE:
I don't see that religion or God has any good. As far as I can see your god is a pretty good excuse for you to write off a lot of injustice. How many innocent people have suffered because they didn't believe the right thing?

TONY:
How do you know they're innocent?

BEATRICE:
Look at the Inquisition.

MARK:
That's ancient history.

BEATRICE:

Doesn't change the fact that people were burned for the most incredible reasons. On the slightest pretext.

MARK:

That was a long time ago.

BEATRICE:

Just answer my question. Did innocent people die because they didn't believe the right thing?

MARK:

Those people were heretics, Bea. The Church was responsible for the overall well-being and safety of the society. They couldn't have a bunch of lunatics running around doing whatever they wanted.

BEATRICE:

Perfectly innocent people are always—

MARK:

There is no such thing. Force is required to keep order. Look at Southeast Asia after the Americans left. Look at—

BEATRICE:

That is the biggest over-simplification—

MARK:

No it's not. Those are the facts. Facts. You know what your problem is?

BEATRICE:

No. Tell me.

MARK:

You don't believe in anything. I don't mean just God. You don't believe that anything is absolutely true. You believe that everyone is equal and—

BEATRICE:

Everyone is equal.

MARK:

Everybody's equal and has equal rights and can believe whatever they want and everybody can do whatever they want and everything cancels everything out. Everything is relative and we should put up, pardon me, tolerate anything anybody does or believes because we're all equal and there's no such thing as Truth or Good or ...

Well, that doesn't work. I think that's become pretty clear.

BEATRICE:

I have no idea what you're talking about.

She and TONY laugh.

MARK:

If you were an administrator—a British administrator when the English were in India would you have allowed the natives to burn their wives?

BEATRICE:

The English should never have been in India.

MARK:

Best thing ever happened to India and you're not answering my question. Would you have stopped their ritual, interfered with their religion or whatever it is, imposed your beliefs, bearing in mind that the woman wants to die and be with her husband? (*Silence.*) You see you can't answer that question because you don't have any absolutely solid values to help you make your decision.

BEATRICE:

And you do?

MARK:

Yes. I do. Fortunately some of us still do. You can go on and on about the Inquisition and perfectly innocent people. If the world was left in the hands of all those innocent, equal people it would be total chaos. It's very easy to sit here and judge those things but you don't have any right to judge. None.

BEATRICE:

Who does?

MARK:

God. God has the right.

Scene 16

BEATRICE:

There are four other nominations. And I'm going to win, I know it. I'm going to go up there and say, "This proves that there are still people out there with imaginations and a sense of humour." After all the stupid arguments I've had over this thing—with staff, the client even. And you know the funny thing—this ad isn't even that good. I've done better.

TONY:

Great.

BEATRICE:

It is great. I'm going to rub their faces in it.

TONY:

Cheap revenge.

BEATRICE:

It's not revenge.

TONY:

Yes it is. You want to rub their faces in it.

BEATRICE:

So what? I've said time and time again that the marketplace alone should decide what works.

TONY:

I know.

BEATRICE:

And I'm right. I'm going to win for a design that everybody thought was too risky. Risk. They wouldn't know a goddamned risk if it jumped up and bit them in the ass. This award proves—

TONY:
You haven't won yet.

BEATRICE:
I will.

TONY:
We'll see.

BEATRICE:
You don't think I'll win?

TONY:
I don't know.

BEATRICE:
You okay?

TONY:
Sure.

BEATRICE:
No you're not. What's wrong?

TONY:
Nothing.

BEATRICE:
Come on. Tell me what's up.

She goes to him and begins to tickle him.

I have ways of making you talk you know.

TONY:
(*pulls away violently*) Jesus Bea, don't.

BEATRICE:
What's wrong with you?

TONY:
Nothing. What's wrong with you?

BEATRICE:
Nothing. There's nothing wrong with me.

Scene 17

MARIA calls again.

MARIA:
Is he home?

BEATRICE:
He's not in. What do you want?

MARIA:
I want my sister.

BEATRICE:
Your sister.

MARIA:
Tell him that time is running out.

BEATRICE:
What do you mean?

MARIA:
Who are you?

BEATRICE:
His wife.

MARIA:
His wife.

BEATRICE:
Perhaps I can be of some help ...

MARIA:
I doubt it.

BEATRICE:
Who are you?

MARIA:
My name is Maria. That's all he needs to know.

BEATRICE:
Can we meet somewhere Maria?

Scene 18

A public park.

MARIA:
(*from a distance*) Hello.

BEATRICE:
Are you—

MARIA:
Stay where you are. Keep your hands by your side.

BEATRICE:
I'm Beatrice. How do you know Tony?

MARIA:
Don't move. You're his wife.

BEATRICE:
Yes. What do you want from him?

MARIA:
He has my sister.

BEATRICE:
What do you mean?

MARIA:
Do you know what your husband does? Professionally?

BEATRICE:
Yes.

MARIA:
Do you? He's told you about it while you're having dinner. About the electric shocks, the cattle prod? You know about the blow torch?

BEATRICE:
What are you talking about?

MARIA:
He hasn't told you.

BEATRICE:
Why did you ask me to meet you?

MARIA:
I didn't.

BEATRICE:
You agreed to meet me. Why?

MARIA:
Because I want my sister back—because I'm a fucking idiot.
Tell your husband that I will kill him. I will.

BEATRICE:
Who are you?

MARIA:
Who are you?

Scene 19

The Box.

TONY:
I'm very sorry. I'm disappointed. I've tried to be patient. My
friend, he's not quite so patient. He's not very patient at all.
I'm sorry.

MARK:
"For the day of the Lord is near upon all the heathen; as thou
hast done, it shall be done to thee."

Scene 20

BEATRICE and TONY in bed.

TONY:
It's weird.

BEATRICE:
Yes.

TONY:

That's never happened before.

BEATRICE:

Never?

TONY:

No. Maybe it's broken.

BEATRICE:

Broken?

TONY:

Sure, if you use something too much it wears down. It breaks.

BEATRICE:

I don't think we use it enough.

TONY:

Could be. It's atrophied.

BEATRICE:

What should we do?

TONY:

We either get a new one or we get this one fixed.

BEATRICE:

Probably cheaper to get a new one.

TONY:

Probably.

BEATRICE:

We'll throw this one out and get a new one. Poor Mr. McThingy.

TONY:

Everyone has their off days.

BEATRICE:

It's probably an easy operation. They just cut this one off and sew a new one on. Maybe we can choose different sizes and styles.

TONY:
Okay. That's enough.

BEATRICE:
Maybe we should try something different. (*Silence.*) I don't know. Maybe we're boring. We need some variety. If you want to … try something kinky … I don't mind.

TONY:
What?

BEATRICE:
I could tie you up. Or, I dominate people all day, maybe I'm too aggressive. If you want to spank me … I wouldn't mind.

TONY:
You wouldn't mind.

BEATRICE:
Or I've heard that there are screws you can put on your nipples. You go beyond the pain after a while.

TONY:
Hit me. Get my belt. Go on. Hit me with it.

She does.

Not like that. Fold it over in half. Hit me hard on my back.

She does.

Yes. Again. Faster.

She does.

Harder. Hit me.

After a dozen or so blows she stops.

BEATRICE:
Are you hard?

TONY:
Yes.

Scene 21

The office—MARK on phone.

MARK:

Hi sweetheart. Hello, helloooo. What's that? I don't think so.
I'm sorry, but for Christmas … I promise we'll spend the
whooole holiday together. Okay? Promise. How's school?
You're having a bore. That's because you're too smart. What's
that? You're not too smart … the teachers are dumbos. I see.
Dumbos and bumbos. Is your mother there? Okay. I love you
too. Bye-bye.

What? No. I said I can't take her this weekend. I'm too busy.
Well, you'll have to take her with you for once. Diane—I just
told—she stays with me for Christmas. God damn you woman.
(hangs up phone)

TONY:

Trouble?

MARK:

She's going on some Buddhist retreat or something this
weekend and then she says I can't have Annie for Christmas.
Fuck. She's my kid too. I pay for the fucking private school
she goes to.

TONY:

Want to go for a drink?

MARK:

No. Thanks.

TONY:

I'll buy.

MARK:

You're buying? Are you feeling okay?

TONY:

All right.

MARK:

I better write this one down. What day is it?

TONY:
Do you want to go for a drink or not?

MARK:
Thanks, but we've got work to do.

TONY:
Well, I'm going.

MARK:
Where?

TONY:
For a drink.

MARK:
I'd better come keep an eye on you. Who knows what kind of trouble you'll get into on your own.

Scene 22

TONY and BEATRICE. TONY throwing up.

BEATRICE:
Do the people you question at work give you information of their own free will?

TONY:
… Yes …

BEATRICE:
And if they don't?

TONY:
We threaten them.

BEATRICE:
With what?

TONY:
They don't get any fucking dessert.

BEATRICE:
Do you ever hit them?

TONY:
What?

BEATRICE:
Do you beat them?

TONY:
No.

BEATRICE:
Never?

TONY:
No.

BEATRICE:
Good.

Scene 23

MONICA on sabotage and animals.

MONICA:
One. One, two.

In the Nazi camps the prisoners would try to get jobs in the laundry or the kitchen. And they would perform little acts of sabotage. Burning a shirt, spoiling the soup. Here, there are no laundries or kitchens. Sabotage is almost impossible.

One, two, three.

This is a machine that makes animals. They put us in here and tell us to moo instead of talk.

In the morning, it's almost better to be an animal. The guard comes by and sometimes he speaks to me. He is a stupid brute. I have begun to hope that he will stay a little longer and speak to me for a while. When he offered me a cigarette I almost cried. I mustn't begin to believe he is my friend.

One, two, three, four.

There was someone in this block who could whistle like a bird. Every night she would whistle and we would tap very quietly on the walls when she was finished. And she—I don't know if it was a woman but I like to think so—she would whistle a little more. I'd fall asleep to her whistling.

Whistling, tapping, scratching our names in the wall, counting out loud. This is our sabotage.

Cows can't count.

One, two, three, four, five.

Scene 24

The Box.

MARK:

Now then why don't you tell us where he is? If you just tell us where he is I'll let you go. If you don't I'll have to shoot you. (*pulls out gun*) Ready? You tell me where he is before I count to five and you're free to go, if you don't you're dead. Right? One two, three, four ... five. (*gun clicks*) Ha. (*laughs*) It's not loaded. A little joke. Don't you like jokes?

No.

Now, don't be stupid. We'll find him sooner or later. Don't be a martyr. Tell me where he is. Where is he? You shouldn't be so stupid. (*begins hitting her*) Where is he? Tell me. Where is he? Where is he? (*kicking*) Where is he? (*rolls her over*) Oh shit.

TONY:

What is it?

MARK:

She's out.

Scene 25

Office.

TONY:

What did you do that for?

MARK:

What? Do what?

TONY:

(*grabbing MARK*) What the hell are you trying to do?

MARK:

Hey, hey, what the fuck is—

TONY:

What are you doing? What do you think—

MARK:

My job. I'm doing my job.

> *MARK violently puts TONY down.*

All right? I'm surprised at you, Tony. Disappointed. I
suggested they move you up because I thought you had it
together. Thought you were pretty smart.

TONY:

I didn't know it was going to—

MARK:

You knew what went on.

TONY:

It's different inside. You trying to kill her. She's no good to us
dead. You don't have to do that.

MARK:

Bit late for that, Tony. She's gone. Pull yourself together.
(*Beat.*) Go get the doctor.

Scene 26

TONY's confession.

*TONY with drink. Smokes cigarette. Rolls up sleeve. Burns
forearm with cigarette. Slowly, without sign of pain. Burns himself
again. BEATRICE enters. He goes to burn himself a third time.*

BEATRICE:
Tony!

TONY:
Bea. You scared me.

BEATRICE:
Tony what are you doing?

TONY:
Nothing. Having a drink.

BEATRICE:
I saw you. You burned yourself with that cigarette. Show me
your arm.

She takes his arm; he cries out.

I'll get something to clean it.

TONY:
No, it's fine. It's nothing. Don't bother.

BEATRICE:
What are you trying—what's wrong with you?

TONY:
I just wanted to see what it was like.

Somebody died. At work.

BEATRICE:
Jesus.

TONY:
We killed somebody.

BEATRICE:
Who?

TONY:

A woman.

BEATRICE:

No, who killed her?

TONY:

Mark, I did. She was very weak. We should have left her alone
but the doctor said she could take it. He pumped her up with
some stuff—

BEATRICE:

Take what?

TONY:

Being questioned. Mark hit her.

BEATRICE:

Mark hit her.

TONY:

Yes.

BEATRICE:

Mark. You didn't hit anybody.

TONY:

I was right there. You never go in alone. She fell—Mark hit
her too hard—pushed her. She passed out. She died on us.
There was nothing I could do.

BEATRICE:

You lied to me. You hit people.

TONY:

Whatever is required. We rough them up—if they won't talk.
I've hit people. No one's ever died. We scare them. They were
breathing down our necks for the information.

It's standard procedure. The doctor is there to tell us how far
we can go. It's a war Bea. You don't understand. It's a war and
I'm in it. I didn't choose this. I follow orders.

She just died. That's all. I never killed anybody.

I can't go back. I don't want to go back there.

BEATRICE:
Who was she?

Scene 27

BEATRICE visits *MARIA*.

MARIA:
What are you doing here?

BEATRICE:
I heard about your sister, Monica. I heard about Monica and I just—

MARIA:
You heard what?

BEATRICE:
That she died. I'm very sorry. I just wanted to tell you how sorry—

MARIA:
What is this?

BEATRICE:
I know it must be very difficult. It's very difficult for me. I'd like to talk to you. I knew Monica. We worked together.

MARIA:
You knew Monica?

BEATRICE:
I knew her. I did. I knew her. I knew her.

Scene 28

MARK:
We've all been really worried about you, Tony. Everybody sends their best. How are you feeling?

TONY:
Not too good.

MARK:

What is it Tony? You feel a bit burned out? Everybody's really concerned. What is it?

TONY:

You killed her, Mark.

MARK:

Who? I never killed anybody.

TONY:

That girl. You killed her.

MARK:

She died. It's unfortunate. I didn't kill her.

TONY:

She's dead because you hit her. Nobody ever died before.

MARK:

Not in front of you, you mean. It was an accident. Tony, I know it's hard. You have to trust that we're doing the right thing.

TONY:

I don't.

MARK:

Pinhead wants to know when you're coming back.

TONY:

You can tell Pinhead I'm not coming back.

MARK:

Not right away, he knows. But how much time do you want off?

TONY:

I'm not going back.

MARK:

Pinhead suggested that when you come back we could put you in a different department for a while.

TONY:

No.

MARK:

Maybe I can arrange for some kind of permanent transfer.

TONY:

That's a lousy choice of words.

MARK:

I mean maybe we can arrange for you to be re-assigned.

TONY:

Nothing can be arranged.

MARK:

You think you can just walk away. (*Silence.*) It's not like that, Tony. (*Silence.*) What are you going to do?

TONY:

I don't know. I might go see a psychiatrist or something.

MARK:

A psychiatrist?

TONY:

Or something.

MARK:

Something? You want to talk? Talk to me. I've been through it. I'm the one to talk to.

TONY:

I don't want to talk.

> *Beat.*

MARK:

What are you telling Bea, Tony?

TONY:

Bea? I—that's none of your business.

MARK:

It is though.

Scene 29

TONY:
Bea—Bea where are you?

BEATRICE:
I'm right here. What do you want?

TONY:
Nothing—I—

BEATRICE:
Do you want something to eat?

TONY:
No.

BEATRICE:
You should eat something.

TONY:
I couldn't keep it down.

BEATRICE:
What are you going to do, Tony?

TONY:
What do you mean?

BEATRICE:
What are you going to do? Or do you plan to sit here for the rest of your life?

TONY:
Bea—I'm ...

BEATRICE:
You're what? Sick?

TONY:
Yes I am sick. What's wrong?

BEATRICE:
What?

TONY:
You seem upset.

BEATRICE:
I am. Does that surprise you? What if I told you I didn't work for an ad agency? That I was actually ... a member of the Nazi Party. Would you maybe be a little fucking upset?

TONY:
I work for the government.

BEATRICE:
You kill people.

TONY:
I do not.

BEATRICE:
You lied to me. You lied.

I knew her, Tony. Monica. Monica. She worked for me. I told you about her. How could you not know?

You—I don't even know you. I've loved someone else. Someone who doesn't exist.

TONY:
I'm not somebody else. I'm Tony.

BEATRICE:
Don't. Don't you touch me. Don't you ever touch me again. You'd better decide what you're going to do. I won't have you in my house.

TONY:
You going to throw me out? It's my house too.

What do you know about it? Call me a liar. You've never kept anything from me? Is that it?

You are so fucking selfish. Your house, your life. Fuck you. I'm stuck in this. I didn't choose it.

I do what I have to. What the fuck would you know about it?

BEATRICE:

It is my house, my life. I put it together. By myself. You were too out of it to do anything. You've never had an idea of your own. You're right—you didn't choose this mess. You never chose anything. You just let yourself get swept along by whatever happens.

TONY:

What the fuck would you know about this, Bea? Tell me. What am I supposed to do? There's no way out of this.

BEATRICE:

Go to the police.

TONY:

You don't get it.

BEATRICE:

Turn yourself in. Tell them what happened.

TONY:

The police work for me, Beatrice.

Scene 30

BEATRICE learns that she has won.

BEATRICE:

(*on phone*) I've won. For the ad. Oh. (*Pause.*) Yes, yes, I'm here. I'm shocked. Yes I am pleased. I'm … thrilled. It's very exciting.

From the movies—I don't know which one. You know, war movies. Pardon? Interrogating the product … I don't understand. Oh, like interrogating the prod … Sure you can use that. Well, thank you.

I have to go. I'm sorry. I'm very busy. Yes, I'll be there. Thank you. Goodbye.

Scene 31

BEATRICE phones MARK—7 a.m.

BEATRICE:
Mark? It's Beatrice.

MARK:
Bea. Uh, what—

BEATRICE:
Tony's gone.

MARK:
What?

BEATRICE:
He wasn't home—he hasn't come home. He's been gone
since yesterday afternoon.

MARK:
All right Bea. Just ... stay calm. Do you know if he went
anywhere yesterday?

BEATRICE:
I went to work. I left him. I—he wasn't well.

MARK:
I'll call the hospitals.

BEATRICE:
I've called them already.

MARK:
I'll try again. Don't you worry. I'm sure he'll turn up. (*Silence.*)
Bea?

BEATRICE:
I'm here.

MARK:
Do you want me to come over?

BEATRICE:
No I'm all right.

MARK:
I'll call you as soon as I have something.

Scene 32

BEATRICE and MARK—restaurant.

BEATRICE:
I can't work. I can't do anything.

MARK:
You should try to work. Keep things as normal as possible.

BEATRICE:
Normal. Everything is normal. I walk—I walk down the
street and it's normal. The people, the stores—business as
usual. Normal. The traffic, normal. The noise, normal. I want
to scream everything's so fucking normal.

I want to scream at people—smash things.

I can't stand being in the house.

I keep thinking he'll be there, having a drink. I keep thinking
he'll be there. Every fucking goddamned normal day. I hope
he'll be there.

MARK:
Bea, I know it's hard—

BEATRICE:
No you don't. No one does. Me, I'm alone. Me, I'm scared.
I'm sick with worry. Not knowing if he's alive—I'd give
anything just to know.

MARK:
Bea …

BEATRICE:
I'm sorry Mark. I'm so fucked up. I'm sorry. I didn't mean to
take it out on you.

MARK:
It's all right.

BEATRICE:

I'm such an asshole. If it weren't for you I'd have gone right over the edge by now.

MARK:

I haven't done anything.

BEATRICE:

You've been very supportive through this whole thing.

MARK:

Tony's my friend. I want him to turn up as much as you do.

BEATRICE:

Can I ask you—what do you do at work?

MARK:

We monitor extremist political organizations.

BEATRICE:

How?

MARK:

Bea ... information gathering, surveillance, phone taps, records of all kinds, every method authorized under the Security and ....

BEATRICE:

Do you use force?

MARK:

Force? Bea, didn't Tony ever explain ... ?

We basically push papers ... sort information. Most of these groups are a joke. Culty things with ten members and half of them are our people but a few of them are serious. Big organizations. Maybe into drugs ... guns, industrial sabotage ... there are some very screwed up people with dangerous ideas out there.

BEATRICE:

Where is he?

MARK:

I wish I knew.

BEATRICE:

I know what happened.

MARK:

What happened where?

BEATRICE:

I know.

MARK:

Why don't I take you home?

BEATRICE:

I don't want to go home.

MARK:

I think we should go.

BEATRICE:

No.

MARK:

All right. (*Silence.*) How's your fish?

BEATRICE:

Fine.

MARK:

You should try to eat a bit more. More wine?

Bea, you have to trust me. I know this is a terrible time for you but I'm doing all I can.

I want you to know that you can come to me. I'm your friend. And please be careful ... you know? About who you do talk to. For Tony's sake, I mean. Until we find him. We have to be very cautious.

Scene 33

MARIA remembers the testimonies.

MARIA:

Why don't you ask his buddy—The Preacher?

BEATRICE:
    Preacher?

MARIA:
    The one who works with him—quotes the Bible. Runs the
    place basically.

BEATRICE:
    Mark.

MARIA:
    Yeah.

BEATRICE:
    He's doing everything he can.

MARIA:
    Your husband is in the basement of the Naval School.

BEATRICE:
    How can you know?

MARIA:
    Educated guess. Your husband is being held by the people he
    worked for. He's dangerous; he left.

BEATRICE:
    Tony's not dangerous.

MARIA:
    He is to them.

BEATRICE:
    But Mark and Tony—they are friends.

MARIA:
    Friends? You still don't get it do you? (*Beat.*) I know. I've got
    some reading material for you.

BEATRICE:
    What?

MARIA:
    My sister gave me these. They're testimonies from people who
    have been tortured and released later. Read them—

BEATRICE:

How can you possibly know all this? How can you know what Tony and Mark—

MARIA:

They know about us; we know a few things about them.

BEATRICE:

Who's we?

MARIA:

Doesn't matter. Start reading—there's a lot to get through.

BEATRICE:

I can't—not right now—I don't … I just want to know where my husband is. That's all. I just want to know—if he's alive or …

MARIA:

You know how many times I've heard that the past few years?

BEATRICE:

You don't have an ounce of compassion—you make me sick. Why should I believe anything you say? You're lying. You're playing some game. I don't believe a word of this shit.

Silence.

MARIA:

It's very late. You can stay here tonight if you want. Are you hungry?

Scene 34

MARK alone. On phone. Office.

MARK:

I just don't think it would be effective. It's purely professional. I know it won't work this way. Yes, it is my opinion.

I—there must be—I do the scheduling—don't try to tell me there's no one else available.

No—no, I don't have a problem. It means nothing to me.
Fine. Fine. Instructions from upstairs. Fine.

Yes, I'll go in. Fine.

(*hangs up*) Fuck you. Fuck your instructions. Fuck your
upstairs. Fuck you.

He slowly gathers clipboard, keys, packs gun and exits.

Scene 35

MARIA's bedroom.

MARIA:
> It's not a great pillow. Do you want this one?

BEATRICE:
> No. This is fine. I prefer feather pillows. (*fluffs it*)

MARIA:
> You sure?

BEATRICE:
> Absolutely. (*punches pillow*)

MARIA:
> Okay. (*lights joint*) This is like being ten years old.

BEATRICE:
> Sleeping over.

MARIA:
> Monica and I used to share this bed. We were smaller then.

BEATRICE:
> (*punches pillow*) Do you have enough room?

MARIA:
> I'm fine. Are you?

BEATRICE:
> Fine. (*fluffs pillow*)

MARIA:
> Do you want this pillow?

BEATRICE:

I just have to get this one into the right shape.

MARIA:

Take this one.

BEATRICE:

No, these are better for my neck.

MARIA passes joint.

Thanks. Have you lived here long?

MARIA:

I grew up in this neighbourhood.

BEATRICE:

You've lived here all your life?

MARIA:

No. I lived with a guy on the other side of town for about three years.

BEATRICE:

Do you have an ashtray?

MARIA:

He left the country two years ago and I moved back. (*passes ashtray*)

BEATRICE:

You didn't go with him?

MARIA:

I couldn't see myself living in Sweden.

BEATRICE:

He went to Sweden? (*passes joint*)

MARIA:

Stockholm. I couldn't imagine living in a city that only gets five hours of sunlight.

BEATRICE:

Why Sweden?

MARIA:
France wouldn't take him and a lot of our friends had gone to Sweden so ...

BEATRICE:
We spent—I was in France.

MARIA:
I lived there for a year. (*passing joint*) Finish it.

BEATRICE:
Thanks. Where did you live?

MARIA:
Nanterre. I studied there for a year.

BEATRICE:
You did?

MARIA:
Long story. My mother's family sent us away after my father died.

BEATRICE:
What did he do?

MARIA:
He was a journalist.

BEATRICE:
Did you like Europe?

MARIA:
I didn't see much of it. I loved Rome.

BEATRICE:
Rome. Rome is beautiful. All those pastel colours ...

MARIA:
Do you know the Caffe San Eustachio?

BEATRICE:
Don't think so.

MARIA:
Best coffee in the world.

BEATRICE:
Did you go to the Vatican?

MARIA:
Yes.

BEATRICE:
Did you mail anything from the Vatican post office?

MARIA:
No.

BEATRICE:
I sent some postcards and I swear the stamps tasted just like communion wafers.

MARIA:
Oh yeah.

BEATRICE:
I swear.

MARIA:
Did you go to Eur?

BEATRICE:
What's that?

MARIA:
Suburb, just outside of Rome. Mussolini built it.

BEATRICE:
By himself?

MARIA:
No, his brother Bruno helped. Very weird, ugly in a grand sort of way.

BEATRICE:
I'd love to go back.

MARIA:
Hmmm. Communion wafers.

BEA:
They did. They tasted just like communion wafers.

MARIA:
I'm sure they did.

BEATRICE:
I was so surprised. But it makes sense I guess.

MARIA:
I guess it does. It's late.

BEATRICE:
Is it?

MARIA:
Should get some sleep.

    BEATRICE punches pillow.

Are you going to do that all night?

BEATRICE:
No. It's perfect now.

MARIA:
Communion wafers.

BEATRICE:
It's true.

Scene 36

    The Box.

MARK:
Let's stop fucking around here, Tony.

TONY:
You goddamn son of a—

MARK:
Save it Tony. Tell me what Beatrice is up to.

TONY:
How the hell would I know? I've been in here for—

MARK:
Before that. How long has she known Maria?

TONY:

Maria?

MARK:

You remember Maria. Beatrice has been spending a lot of
time with her. Why?

TONY:

You're lying.

MARK:

Look at these. (*shows him photos*) You know she quit her job?
She's really screwed up. Very worried about you. (*Silence.*)
Why didn't you tell me you'd spoken to this woman?

TONY:

I never spoke to—

MARK:

You had a telephone conversation. Would you like to hear it?
Why didn't you tell us?

TONY:

I didn't believe her—I thought we had—

MARK:

You thought you'd make some decisions on your own? Tell
me about Beatrice and Maria.

TONY:

I don't know anything about—

MARK:

We could drag Bea in here in 20 minutes.

Scene 37

MARIA:

Your husband's colleague, Mark, The Preacher, do you know
him well?

BEATRICE:

Yes.

MARIA:

Can you arrange a meeting?

BEATRICE:

A meeting? Why? (*Silence.*) Kill him. You want to kill him.

MARIA:

We're going to execute him.

BEATRICE:

That's no—violence will only lead to more violence.

MARIA:

Monica used to say that.

BEATRICE:

She was right. Killing Mark will not solve anything.

MARIA:

How many deaths is he responsible for?

BEATRICE:

You don't know that.

MARIA:

He's guilty.

BEATRICE:

What gives you the right to decide who lives and who dies? (*Beat.*) What if I turned you in right now? I could.

MARIA:

You think they don't know we've met? They could pick both of us up at any time.

BEATRICE:

This puts you on exactly the same level as them.

MARIA:

There is a huge difference.

BEATRICE:

I don't see any difference.

MARIA:

You don't see anything. Have you read the stuff I gave you?

BEATRICE:

　No.

MARIA:

　Why not?

BEATRICE:

　I haven't.

MARIA:

　You haven't what? Had the guts?

　You don't see anything and you don't want to know anything. You just want your poor little Tony to come back so you can pretend that nothing ever happened. Your husband tortured people for a living!

　I'll bet you got real worked up over Tiananmen Square. People like you can work up a real fury about problems on the other side of the globe but do you give a shit about what happens in your own backyard?

BEATRICE:

　I don't have to justify myself to you.

MARIA:

　You can't anyway. Can you? You can't. So do something.

BEATRICE:

　What? Murder? That's doing some—

MARIA:

　Set up the meeting.

BEATRICE:

　"Executing" him won't bring your sister back.

MARIA:

　This is not about my sister.

BEATRICE:

　Your sister that you left to die. You knew where she was and you let her die.

　A moment.

MARIA:

Will you set up the meeting?

BEATRICE:

If I do, will you let Tony go?

Scene 38

The Box—TONY is transferred.

MARK:

You're being transferred Tony.

"He that hath no rule over his own spirit is like a city that is broken down and hath no walls." Sorry Tony. Nothing I could do.

Scene 39

MARIA phones BEATRICE.

MARIA:

Your husband is being transferred.

BEATRICE:

Maria.

MARIA:

You won't see him again.

That man, Mark, or the police will phone you some time tonight and tell you that they found his body. They'll find it either at the dock or the garbage dump.

BEATRICE:

You did this—

MARIA:

No. No, believe me ...

BEATRICE:

How ... ?

MARIA:

A friend was released yesterday. He said a group of prisoners were going to be transferred today. Your husband was one of them.

BEATRICE:

How would he know Tony?

MARIA:

He recognized him. Your husband tortured him. And for the last month they've shared a cell.

Scene 40

MARK phones BEATRICE.

BEATRICE:

At the dump.

MARK:

Yeah. Are you okay Bea? (*Silence.*) Do you want me to come over?

BEATRICE:

I want to see his body.

MARK:

Not right away. Why don't I come over?

BEATRICE:

No.

Scene 41

BEATRICE reads the testimonies.

BEATRICE:

P. T. / arrested on the street May 26.

MONICA:

(*overlap*) / Arrested at home February 2.

BEATRICE:
They threw me to the floor in a room where I remained under guard. They told me: / We are very good at what we do.

MONICA:
/ In here we are God.

BEATRICE:
Then came the interrogation session and they began to beat me. / They put electrodes to my head, testicles and feet and began to give me electric shock for about three hours.

MONICA:
They put electrodes to my head, nipples, feet and hands. The blows and interrogation session went on forever.

TONY:
They took me to another room.

BEATRICE:
Where they made me lie on a kind of bed frame.

BEATRICE:
(and TONY) They tied me up and attached electrodes to my head, testicles, chest, feet and hands. They gave me stronger shocks this time.

MONICA:
A guard

BEATRICE:
A policeman

TONY:
A soldier

BEATRICE:
Sprayed water on me.

TONY:
It felt as if my head and whole body were suspended in the air. I lost consciousness.

MONICA:

They woke me up with ammonia to carry on the torture. They filled my mouth with water and put a metal clip on my lips and gave me electric shocks. When I screamed, I swallowed the water and the pain passed through my whole body.

BEATRICE:

They said they would kill my girlfriend and my 12-year-old sister if I didn't say what they wanted.

Scene 42

MARK's funeral oration.

MARK:

We were very lucky to have known Tony. He was kind, considerate. He was a man who was deeply concerned about the world we live in. He was a (*begins to cry*) a—dear friend. He was my friend and—a man who worked to ensure the safety of others was brutally taken from us. As painful as that thought is we must bear it in mind. We must not forget.

"Let me die the death of the righteous and let my last end be like his."

Scene 43

BEATRICE is looking at photographs of herself and MARIA.

BEATRICE:

I was so confused I didn't know who to believe. I must have been a little crazy.

MARK:

I understand.

BEATRICE:

I was … disoriented. That woman seemed so kind. I feel terrible about not trusting you.

MARK:

(*tearing up photos*) It's all over now.

BEATRICE:

I want to thank you for ...

MARK:

We're friends. I did it for Tony and you. I'm glad you've come
around. If you'd gone any farther with that woman ... I don't
know what I could have done if they'd brought you in. It
would have been pretty unpleasant.

BEATRICE:

How unpleasant?

MARK:

I don't imagine it's much fun being locked in a cell.

BEATRICE:

I don't imagine it is. But it's a war isn't it. Isn't it?

MARK:

A war? I—

BEATRICE:

Don't move.

MARK:

What?

BEATRICE:

I said don't move. Stay there.

He moves.

I'm warning you.

MARK:

Bea ... what is wro—

BEATRICE:

I have a gun. I have a—

She reveals it.

MARK:

Beatrice, please. Let's stay calm here.

BEATRICE:

Shut up, don't talk, don't move. What happened to Tony?

MARK:

Bea, I don't know—

BEATRICE:

Did you kill him?

MARK:

No. No, Bea. You've got this—

BEATRICE:

Did you detain him?

MARK:

Bea, I would never—

He gets up slowly.

BEATRICE:

Did you hurt him?

MARK:

Bea please, why don't you put that down?

He is moving towards her.

Give it to me. Just gently. Just—

BEATRICE:

Maria! Maria!

MARIA enters, armed.

MARK:

No! Please.

MARIA shoots. BEATRICE shoots.

Scene 44

Out of the city.

MARIA:
The car should be here soon. Want an orange?

BEATRICE:
Sure.

MARIA:
Isn't this place beautiful? Those are lemon trees. You should
see it when they're in bloom. Lemons, oranges, the smell is
incredible. There used to be an aviary over there. We used to
eat on the patio in the evenings and the birds would talk and
sing as long as we had the lights on but the moment the lights
went off they'd fall asleep. Just like that. We'd sit in the dark
and stare at the stars. Sky's so full of stars out here.

BEATRICE:
It is beautiful. I don't want to leave.

MARIA:
You have to. We're going to claim responsibility this afternoon.

Don't worry. You'll come back. We'll spend a month here.
We'll sleep late and have coffees on the patio. We'll go for
long walks. We'll fix the aviary and pick fresh oranges.

BEATRICE:
When?

MARIA:
Soon. A year or two. You have the passport?

BEATRICE:
Yes. And the testimonies.

MARIA:
You're taking them? You think the truth will set us free?
Everybody knows everything. The worst is normal now. What
do you think you're going to do with those?

BEATRICE:

I don't know. I don't know. Right now, I'm just tired. I really want to go away and forget. I don't know why I'm taking them. I want to forget everything.

MARIA:

We can't forget. We have to remember. Never forget and never forgive. (*Silence.*) Don't worry. Everything is going to be fine. You've got the passport?

BEATRICE:

Yes, you asked me already. Passport, money.

MARIA:

You'll be back soon. Sometimes you can see flamingoes flying past here. You'll see them when you come back.

BEATRICE:

Yes I will.

MARIA:

We'll all be here waiting for you.

A long silence.

There's the car. You'd better go. Here. (*hands her oranges*) For the trip.

THE END

bloom

bloom was first produced by Modern Times Stage Company at the Theatre Centre in Toronto from February 25 to March 19, 2006 with the following cast and crew:

THE BOY . . . . Anita Majumdar
GERONTION . . . . Andrew Scorer
BARTENDER . . . . Simon Casanova
YOUNG GERONTION /
WAR VETERAN . . . . Peter Farbridge
MARIE . . . . Stavroula Logothettis
TATTERDEMALION WOMAN . . . . . Beatriz Pizano

Director: Soheil Parsa
Lighting designer: Andrea Lundy
Composer: Thomas Ryder Payne
Costumes: Angela Thomas
Stage manager: Elaine Lumley

Author's Note

The Boy is not a boy, but a young man, at least 15 years old. I feel he should be played by a young woman and that no special effort should be made to disguise her, but this is not strictly necessary.

I have borrowed names, phrases, and lines from T. S. Eliot, Samuel Beckett, and others. The War Veteran's Speech is taken from reports given by pilots who bombed the road out of Basra in the 1991 Gulf War.

Some of this material was initially developed with Modern Times Theatre through a collaborative exploratory process. I am very grateful to Soheil Parsa and the actors: Jacquie Burroughs, Ron Kenall, Beatriz Pizano, Michelle Polak, Ken Puley, Yashoda Ranganathan, and Andrew Scorer for their assistance. I would also like to thank: Elizabeth Dancoes, Dennis Foon, Kathryn Kelly, Iris Turcotte, and, especially, Tamsin Kelsey.

This play is for Gary Hobson.

Blessèd art thou, No One.
In thy sight would
we bloom.
In thy
spite.

—Paul Celan

The sound of digging. A group of MOURNERS. A bit of song.

MOURNERS:
Pray for
this is the life
all he consumed
this is the life
all she produced
this is the life
all his goods
this is the life
all her services
this is the life
For now is the time
this is the kingdom
The one and the only
Oh well

♪ ♪ ♪

GERONTION plays harmonica. The BOY listens to the harmonica, from afar. A dog barks. GERONTION stops playing for a moment. The BOY is still. GERONTION listens. The BOY holds his breath. GERONTION begins playing again. The BOY draws nearer. Slowly, creeping. GERONTION half-listens. Keeps playing. The BOY rises, drawn to the harmonica. He approaches GERONTION. GERONTION stops playing. The BOY stands regarding him.

GERONTION:
So.

The BOY stands still.

You're … Come in.

Silence.

I know you're there. I heard you. I can see you there, a
shadow among shadows.

An uneasy silence.

Why don't you ... ?

A moment of silence.

BOY:
What's that?

GERONTION:
What?

BOY:
That sound in your mouth.

GERONTION:
My harmonica?

BOY:
What?

GERONTION:
A harmonica. Do you want to see it?

He holds the harmonica out. The BOY does not move.

Hungry?

BOY:
I heard that song. Do it again.

GERONTION:
It was random ... I don't know what I played exactly.

He plays something approximating the first melody.

BOY:
Tell me again.

GERONTION:
Harmonica.

BOY:
How I came.

GERONTION:
Again?

BOY:
Tell it.

GERONTION:
Why don't you come closer?

The BOY does not move.

There had been thunder, thunder but no rain, naturally. I knew there was something, someone in the field. I'd known for some time. I called out, you said nothing. Perhaps you didn't hear me? I said, "Go, there's nothing here for you." Later, it was cold, I remember, I heard you coming closer. In the house. There was a noise. Particular sort of sound that humans make, different from the scuttling noise of the rat, or—

The BOY moves closer.

BOY:
Tell the story.

GERONTION:
I called boldly, "Stand and unfold yourself."

The BOY stands still.

And you didn't say a word, but I could hear you feel you moving slowly as if trying to get around me behind me. You were afraid.

BOY:
Why?

GERONTION:
Why, the strangeness of it all. The majesty. You were filled with dread. An appropriate sense of awe. And that's when I knew.

BOY:
What?

GERONTION:
That … that you would stay. I welcomed you to Rat's Alley.

BOY:

I was alone?

GERONTION:

Yes.

BOY:

I was wet.

GERONTION:

How?

BOY:

You said.

GERONTION:

No. Thunder, but no rain.

BOY:

When?

GERONTION:

Hard to say. I lose track. Some time.

BOY:

Why don't I remember?

No answer.

Nobody comes here?

GERONTION:

You came.

BOY:

Why can't I remember?

GERONTION:

Remembering is overrated. Won't solve anything. Believe me.

BOY:

I was wet.

GERONTION:

Impossible.

BOY:

You said.

GERONTION:

Don't worry. You're here now. You fell out of the dirty sky like a rock. Flew too close to the sun. You lost your way nel mezzo del cammin di vostra vita, you stumbled into darkness[1] and here you are. We manage, don't we? We get along. Two peas. Bugs in rugs. End of story.

BOY:

End?

✢ ✢ ✢

BOY:

You never had nobody? No old lady to bring you shit, poke the fire, make tea?

GERONTION:

Another life.

BOY:

How did you get here?

GERONTION:

This was my house. Dukedom large enough.

BOY:

You never left.

GERONTION:

Oh yes. I went to war.

BOY:

You?

GERONTION:

I was younger. It was a duty. For everyone.

BOY:

That what happened to your leg?

---

1. Dante, *Inferno.*

GERONTION:

They came raging over us. In the salt marshes and on the banks of the Tigris. And that Turk was on me before I—I deflected the blow and his bayonet—rusted I remember— down and in it went, I watched, as if from a great distance, watched it sink into my thigh, deep, and I thought, well, I'll never run with the bulls again. And that was the beginning of the end.

Hurts today though. Worse today. The cold.

BOY:

You were a soldier?

GERONTION:

It was different. We had ... They were enemies. Others. It was a kind of self-defence. There were two sides, well, not exactly. Two competing ideas. It was clear cut. In a way. Not like now. Not like the jets. We had our orders, rules of engagement. When we flew, it was—

BOY:

You dropped fire?

GERONTION:

It was different. Another life. Another world.

A beat.

I have something. Look.

He holds out his hand.

BOY:

What?

GERONTION:

Seeds.

The BOY pokes them.

BOY:

Like in stories? Jack Giant Killer.

GERONTION:

Apple, maybe. All plants had seeds before, not just the weeds. Found them in a tin. Take them. Plant them. See if they still work.

BOY:

What?

GERONTION:

Bury them.

BOY:

Why?

GERONTION:

Something might grow.

The BOY finds this funny.

That's how it worked. When I was a boy.

BOY:

In the City.

GERONTION:

In the gardens.

A dog barking.

The cities then were—they stretched over us in a maternal embrace. The world was once a beautiful place, my boy. You can have no idea. Before the Factory and the Automobile, before Monsanto Blight, before the Wars. Before ... A garden it was. (*Pause.*) Not, strictly speaking, entirely accurate, you realize, you understand I poeticize, exaggerate for effect, to make myself look and feel grand. No, the world was ever fucked. Once, perhaps, before we slid from the protozoic slime. Maybe then it was the fabled garden we hear tell of in tales. Ah nostalgia. Oh, before: oh happy lie.

'Tis an unweeded garden, things rank and gross in nature, etc etc. That's what we are, boy. Humans is Weeds. Ugly but hardy and highly adaptive. Like the rats brown and black and red, like the cheatgrass and the thistle, in every bit of the blasted landscape, impossible to eradicate no matter how hard we try.

A dog barks.

Cold today. Remember winter? The obliviating snow, the chestnuts. How warm we were then.

☙ ☙ ☙

Jets roar overhead. GERONTION with a book on his lap. The BOY crumpled in a heap nearby.

GERONTION:
Not for us. Not for us. Do not be afraid. No one cares for us here. We make no difference: we two specks of carbon-based life here. Give me your hand, mouse. Where are you? All right listen then. Where did we leave off?

GERONTION thinks for a moment, then begins to recite.

"The veteran king sat down on the cliff-top. He was sad at heart, unsettled yet ready, sensing his death. His fate hovered near, unknowable but certain ... "[2]

Another jet roars over, obliterating sight and sound. GERONTION clutches the BOY to him.

☙ ☙ ☙

An enthusiastic round of paper, scissors, rock.

☙ ☙ ☙

GERONTION alone. Humming to himself. Then ...

GERONTION:
Shall we play chess?

---

2. *Beowulf*, Seamus Heaney, 165.

104

Silence.

Shall I tell you a story? What are—

He listens hard.

Where are you?

He wheels himself around a moment, listens in various locations, can't hear the BOY anywhere. He grows nervous.

What are you doing?

He calls out loudly.

WHERE ARE YOU?

Nothing. Silence, then the BOY bursts in, oblivious to GERONTION.

GERONTION:
Where were you?

BOY:
Out.

GERONTION:
Outside?

BOY:
Yeah.

GERONTION:
Why?

BOY:
Doing something.

GERONTION:
What something? Is there someone ... there? Outside?

The BOY is fiddling with something in a corner.

BOY:
No. Never no one nowhere. Not here most of all.

A moment.

GERONTION:
What's it like?

BOY:

Out?

GERONTION:

Yes, outside. How is it?

BOY:

Fucked.

GERONTION:

No change then.

An electrical hum is heard. The BOY goes back out.

Where—what are you … ?

Lights and lamps suddenly go on in the room. From the room next door, a TV comes on. The BOY appears.

BOY:

HA! Look, look! Haha!

GERONTION senses the change.

GERONTION:

What? What is it? What have you done?

BOY:

Look. Light. Lights.

He runs off to see the TV.

(*off*) HA! Look! It works! It works.

He comes back in. Picks up a lamp, pulls the shade off and carries it over to GERONTION. He passes the bare bulb very close to his face.

Stole power from the grid. Wired us in.

A pause.

Why'n't you ever fix it?

GERONTION:

No need.

BOY:

You don't know how.

A pause.

How long's been dark?

GERONTION:
Some time.

Lights flare up then out. (In all subsequent scenes one lamp can be on and the TV or radio.)

BOY:
Ah.

GERONTION:
What is it?

The BOY goes out again but GERONTION stops him.

Wait. What is that smell?

BOY:
What?

GERONTION:
From you, the smell is on you.

BOY:
Me? Dirt?

GERONTION:
No, this is some other ... Come here.

The BOY moves closer.

GERONTION:
Closer.

The BOY moves closer. GERONTION pulls the BOY close and smells him intently.

Oh.

Flowers?

The BOY struggles.

BOY:
Let me—

GERONTION:
  Be still.

  He sniffs again.

  There is a burst of sound. Tolling bells. A voice whispers.

  Sound stops suddenly.

  GERONTION drops the BOY's arm. The BOY goes out.
  GERONTION listens and senses around the room.

  ❧ ❧ ❧

  Tolling bells.

  A crowd flows over London Bridge. Individuals in the crowd carry
  bags from Home Depot and the Gap. The crowd organizes itself
  into dancing couples at times, then huddles together, then staggers
  along.

  A jet roars past overhead. The crowd looks up to see the jet. the
  jet passes by and they continue on their way. GERONTION
  comes face to face with the crowd. The crowd breaks up and flows
  around him. A woman, MARIE, steps out of the crowd to face
  him.

GERONTION:
  You.

  She smiles at him.

MARIE:
  Surprise.

  Silence.

GERONTION:
  Are you here?

MARIE:
  I was in the garden.

GERONTION:

The garden? Yes. Your hair wet and your arms full of flowers.
You've come?

MARIE:

Yes, this was my house. I have a life here too. My poems, my
books. The garden.

GERONTION:

How? Is it the boy?

MARIE:

Boy?

GERONTION:

He's here now.

MARIE:

Now? All our efforts paid off then. Took a little longer than
expected.

A silence.

Surely you remember? I do. Those cold thin needles,
harvesting they called it. Even sedated it hurt like hell.

Silence.

GERONTION:

No. This isn't—you? Marie?

MARIE:

Yes.

GERONTION:

But ...

MARIE:

You thought I'd fallen out of the world. It's not like that.

GERONTION:

Like what? I don't understand.

MARIE:

You think time moves only in one direction? You called me.
Across the river.

GERONTION:

How did you get in? I told him to shut the gate!

MARIE:

You still believe it's that simple? You shut the gate, turn your back, practice forgetting. You can barely wipe your own ass, you think you can order everything, everyone to your liking?

GERONTION:

I can wipe my ass perfectly well, thank you.

MARIE:

Let's not argue. I didn't come to argue. We had too much of that.

She comes closer to him.

GERONTION:

Why have you come?

MARIE:

You called me.

GERONTION:

I'm still on this side of the river.

A change in the light. The BOY appears.

BOY:

What's wrong? What is it?

GERONTION:

Her. There.

He points to where MARIE appeared. (She is in another corner.)

BOY:

A ghost? There's nobody else, just us.

GERONTION:

Listen. Don't you hear it?

BOY:

What? Nothing. A dream.

GERONTION:

I wasn't sleeping.

The BOY takes GERONTION by the arm to lead him back to his chair.

The dog barks; GERONTION sniffs the BOY's hand again. Rejects it.

GERONTION:
   Why did you come?

BOY:
   I heard you. I woke—

GERONTION:
   Go.

   Leave my house. Go!

   GERONTION is trying to grab the BOY, hit him.

   I need nothing you're selling. Take yourself, the smell of you, your voice like a bloated vernal day, and GO!

   He throws something at the BOY.

BOY:
   Why? You got lots here.

GERONTION:
   I'm fine. We are fine. The rats and the thistle and I. We have no need of you, stirring—

BOY:
   You. I could break your fucking neck like a stick, strip your guts like a cat.

   Silence.

   I been here so long. Why you want me to go now?

   The dog barks.

   You found me. Coulda left me.

   I wired us in.

GERONTION:
   See what you've dragged in.

   The BOY produces a pill.

111

BOY:

Here.

And puts it in GERONTION's hand.

Eat this.

GERONTION sniffs the pill.

Take it. So we can sleep.

GERONTION:

There's no one else here?

BOY:

No. No one comes here.

GERONTION:

The body of Christ.

GERONTION takes the pill.

෨ ෨ ෨

*GERONTION asleep in his chair. The BOY watches him a
moment. Turns on a lamp. The BOY moves quietly around the
room. Picks up books, opens them, fans the pages, shakes them.
He finds, perhaps in a book, some photographs. He looks at them.
Replaces them in the book. He picks up GERONTION's
harmonica; tentatively blows a note or two. Looks to
GERONTION. Slips harmonica into his pocket. He looks
around. Picks up one of the many books lying about. Stares at a
page or two, turns it one way then the other. Twists his face up as
if trying to form words. He makes little sounds, perhaps imitative
of GERONTION. He grows bored. Tosses the book back to the
ground.*

GERONTION:

Find what you were looking for?

The BOY nudges some books with his foot.

BOY:

What are all these?

GERONTION:

Books. Stories.

BOY:

Why?

GERONTION:

Why?

BOY:

So many.

GERONTION:

Ah. Well, they're each different. In a way.

BOY:

Stories. What for? What good is so many stories?

GERONTION:

They told us something about our lives, about the meaning and purpose and conduct of ...

He begins to laugh.

We used to argue about them even. Used to actually ... They also burn well. Start a good fire. Tell me one of your stories.

BOY:

Don't have stories.

GERONTION:

Of course you do. Man is the animal that makes stories.

BOY:

No.

GERONTION:

Try.

The BOY thinks, remembers something perhaps.

BOY:

Which way is the City?

GERONTION:

The City?

BOY:

How did I get here? Tell me.

GERONTION:

Oh god.

BOY:

Tell me.

GERONTION:

Do you know my nose was completely clogged all night. Had to leave my maw hanging open like some creature of the deep in order to breathe. And we thought living longer was going to be wonderful. Ha! Apothanein thelo!

BOY:

Tell.

GERONTION:

No. It makes no difference. Speak of something else.

A pause.

I lost a little more of my sight in the night.

BOY:

Soon, you'll be all blind. Your fault. In the City they have medicine for that.

GERONTION:

They have medicine for everything. "Wake up you fools. You're on earth; there's no cure for that."

A moment.

No response. Not even a snort of recognition, a hum of interest? Nothing. What's the point of an education if there's no one to share it with, eh? You dog. That's what learning is for: to make little jokes, to pass the time. I say something that you recognize and you offer me a little something that I'll recognize. The bits are the same but we keep rearranging them in different orders, different patterns, right? It's endlessly satisfying.

Silence.

Conversation? A word in the dark?

BOY:

You talk so much noise.

GERONTION:

I do what I can.

BOY:

Tell me.

GERONTION:

I don't remember.

BOY:

You do. One day, you won't remember nothing.

GERONTION:

Is that meant to be a curse? That's how it happens. You forget.
And so you go on. I started to forget to put in my drops, and
so I lost more and more of my sight. That's what it means to
be human, you monkey.

BOY:

Ah! What it means is an accident. Nobody told you? It's on
TV. Human is a survival machine. Just happened over time,
out of an accident, this way. You're only an accident.

GERONTION:

And you?

BOY:

You been alone so long, you still believing superstitions. Souls.
You living in the dark here till I came.

GERONTION:

Oh I know. Let there be light you said and there was ... not
that I can see it, but still ... I believe.

BOY:

Tell me the story!

GERONTION:

Why?

BOY:

I want to know.

GERONTION:

Why such a keen interest in your origins?

BOY:

I want to know how I came.

GERONTION:

So you'll know where to go?

BOY:

Arrrh. Old shit. You old shitty arsefuckmouth. Your tongue a dirty snake in that dark hole in the middle of your face. Your words ... You don't know. You old. You don't know anything anymore and one day you'll be less.

GERONTION:

To be even less than I am already. Is that possible?

BOY:

You'll shit words not joined to nothing.

GERONTION:

Let me tell you about the accident. Open you arms, fling them wide. Yes?

He demonstrates.

Wiggle the fingers on your left hand. That, let us say, represents the beginning of all life on our once blue and green planet. There. The fingers on your left hand.

And now your right hand. The fingers. The tip of your middle finger there, that is today, this unrepeatable, irredeemable moment, this breath, this heart beat? It's a time line from the left hand to the right. You understand? Grunt if you do.

The BOY growls.

Very good.

So, from the middle finger on your left hand all the way to your right shoulder, past your right shoulder, for ages and ages, life is simply bacteria. Around your right elbow, come multi-celled invertebrates. Marvellous trilobites. And so on. Dinosaurs: terrible lizards, appear in the middle of your right palm and pass away at the last joint in your scrawny finger.

116

Humans, upright, bicameral brains, fire-bearing, tool-making, and so on up to whatever it is we are today, all human history accounts for less than a dirty fingernail you tear off with your teeth.[3]

I speak some science, ape.

I've seen the meaningless bones of the long dead. Heard the dry rattle, signifying nothing, when they are disturbed.

I know about the accident.

A moment.

BOY:

Tell me?

GERONTION:

You are persistent.

BOY:

Tell me.

GERONTION:

The story of your piteous appearance on my crumbling doorstep? How you hovered between the reeds, your basket gently nudging the river bank and so on? I have told you. Many times.

BOY:

You. I'll leave you at night, when the ghosts come, I'll just leave you alone. Your broken voice. Calling in the dark, for nothing and no one.

GERONTION:

Listen then, you fiend. Listen. You startled me. Obviously. Obviously, I was startled by your sudden appearance. The intrusion. I dared not move. I asked why you had come. I asked if you'd come by train or plane or photograph: all the ritual questions, for which you gave no answer. I asked whence you'd come and you, in a doubtful, hesitant voice, said—

---

3. Richard Dawkins, *Unweaving the Rainbow.*

Pause.

BOY:

The City.

GERONTION:

New York Berlin Montreal Kandahar.

BOY:

What?

GERONTION:

GO! I said. I thought I could scare you off.

BOY:

I can do things, bring you things, for you.

GERONTION:

I don't need—

BOY:

Be your eyes.

GERONTION:

A man needs not eyes to see how things go in this world.

BOY:

And I asked you to let me stay?

GERONTION:

And I asked what you could do. "Can you play chess? Can you read?" And you said, "I can learn."

A pause.

I thought: A boy. Surely some revelation is at hand.[4] You asked, "What is this place? This stuff?" And I, rather cleverly, replied, "The best that is known and thought." I laughed and welcomed you to Rat's Alley. I may have tossed you a potato. I don't remember. That, more or less, is how it was.

---

4. W. B. Yeats, "The Second Coming."

BOY:

I hardly spoke, you said. You said I was wet, drowned, full fathoms. You said I was scared. You knew I was.

GERONTION:

I don't remember. It was cold. I heard you, felt you. I was afraid. You were afraid. I sensed your dread and incomprehension and Orpheus-like I sang to you, I plucked my lyre and sang.

The BOY has moved closer to GERONTION. Adjusts the blanket around GERONTION's knees and lays his head on GERONTION's lap. GERONTION pats the BOY's head and prepares to sing, hums, coughs, finds his note.

Oh, the cabin boy, the cabin boy, the dirty little nipper. He stuffed his bum with bubble gum and circumcised the skipper.

The BOY joins in.

TOGETHER:

Oh, the cabin boy, the cabin boy, the dirty little nipper. He stuffed his ass with broken glass and circumcised the skipper!

The song repeats, growing more complicated and intricate. Laughter. Then—

BOY:

Is that how it was? Like you said?

A moment.

GERONTION:

It doesn't matter. Our yesterdays. How we came to be here and now. It doesn't. It makes no difference. We just are. As you say: accidents. Doesn't mean anything but it's a comfort to be here just the same.

ↄ ↄ ↄ

MARIE brushes her hair. GERONTION observes her with trepidation. The BOY studies photographs. He brings photos to GERONTION, takes a lamp with him.

BOY:

Who?

GERONTION:

Some indistinguishable and long dead blur.

BOY:

But who? These pictures, so many … pictures. What was this?
Who—

GERONTION:

Dust. (*Beat.*) My gums hurt. Are they bleeding?

> *The BOY looks.*

BOY:

No.

GERONTION:

Are you lying?

> *A silence.*

BOY:

What are all these … ?

GERONTION:

Seemed important at the time.

BOY:

Here. Two heads together. Two people. Shouting? This one. A
crowd. In a circle. Faces wide open. A woman in the middle.
There's something, little—I don't know—bits of shit in the
air, falling? Faces like surprised or … and big eyes. Are they
trying to catch the stuff or throwing? This man beside her …
You? When is this?

> *No answer.*

A road? A broken up road? Why is this a picture? Where are
the people? Is this a road with … what is—falling over
trucks? Where are they going?

GERONTION:

Enough. Enough of your interminable questions. Stirring
everything up. I have no idea. I can't see. I don't know. I do

not know. My back hurts. I can't feel my legs. Bring me a
blanket. Put those away and bring me a blanket.

↢ ↢ ↢

*A pub. People drinking. A BARTENDER wiping glasses. Smoke.
The WAR VETERAN (a young GERONTION) sits in his chair,
the centre of attention. People come up to chat and pay their
respects. They buy him drinks, which MARIE lifts to his lips.
Dancing. And a couple fucking. The strains of "I Could Have
Danced All Night".*

WAR VETERAN:

We dive out of the clouds and the picture is absolutely
astounding. Thousands of headlights on every road that leads
north out of the City. There are vehicles everywhere. It is a
very lucrative target. Innumerable vehicles all heading north.

We drop our three bombs and it's a perfect delivery. The
bombs detonate in a string right across the highway with the
centre bomb in between two trucks, causing both of the
trucks to burst into flame.

BARTENDER:

Time.

WAR VETERAN:

There's a traffic jam beginning and I can see cars pulled off to
the side of the road. Some headlights on, some headlights off.
There's significant gunfire coming from that area, but random,
firing injudiciously, in all directions. So I pick a spot in front of
us that looks like it has the highest concentration of that traffic
jam and we drop three bombs on that. I come up very hard
because the shooting erupts in front of us, even before the
bombs explode. Once the bombs explode, again, other lights
go out, other headlights go out, for miles in every direction.
They're hiding. Don't want to be targeted. Understandably.

BARTENDER:

Last call.

WAR VETERAN:

Behind me, I hear … chuckling, so I called out, Sweeney, you old ape, what's so amusing? I don't believe it, I don't believe it. What? They've turned their headlights back on he says. Look. And I looked up from the targeting pod to glance out the canopy, and, to my astonishment, sure enough, all the headlights were blazing on the road again. It was like turning on the kitchen light late at night and the cockroaches started scurrying … We finally got them out where we could find them and squash them.[5]

BARTENDER:

Time please.

WAR VETERAN:

When I saw the photographs, I was impressed. I admit it. I allowed myself a moment of pride. We were the first to go in and hit that road and we bottled up that traffic and that allowed the rest of the aircraft to go in and do their work. I felt a sense of accomplishment, having achieved the objectives of our mission. I didn't feel any tremendous, um, guilt or anything like that. I felt a sense of accomplishment having flown that mission.

BARTENDER:

Good night.

> *MARIE gets up. Leaves the WAR VETERAN.*

MARIE:

Good night, ladies, good night, sweet ladies, good night, good night.

> *She distributes flowers and goes to drown herself in the river.*

> *An Elizabethan song and the sound of water. Then, the sounds of drowning. Water rising and air escaping. More and more water. Music. GERONTION grows increasingly agitated. He throws his cup and it smashes. The BOY comes in.*

---

5. Marine Lieutenant Colonel Dick White, qtd in *Newsday* (Feb. 1, 1991), 4.

They play paper, scissors, rock. Each time, the BOY announces what he has "thrown," sometimes telling the truth and sometimes lying. Eventually the BOY stops playing.

GERONTION:
Had enough?

The BOY gets up.

Oh, the cabin boy, the cabin boy ... how about a little song then? The Cabin Boy ...

The BOY wanders off to another room. The television comes on.

We are at least two thousand years behind the times. We haven't gotten anywhere at all and we have no sense—look at you—of the past. All we do is philosophize, drink vodka, or complain of boredom.

The BOY returns.

BOY:
What if I ... go ...

GERONTION:
Go?

BOY:
To the City.

GERONTION:
Go? You who begged me for some clean straw in a corner?

BOY:
I did?

GERONTION:
No. I don't think so.

BOY:
Are you my father?

A moment.

GERONTION:

> You know I'm not.

BOY:

> Yeah. But … maybe …
>
> *A pause that the wind fills.*
>
> When the roads were good. When the roads were cleared we left. And … we got lost or … because I wasn't alone.

GERONTION:

> You're not alone now.

BOY:

> There were more of us. Lots of.
>
> *A silence, except for the television muttering in the other room.*

GERONTION:

> Why return to the City?

BOY:

> To find out. To see.

GERONTION:

> What? There is nothing to learn, believe me. Look …
>
> *He indicates the scattered books.*
>
> What will you do in the City if you survive the journey? Sell your organs if Babylon doesn't take them first?

BOY:

> Lies. Story tales.

GERONTION:

> Perhaps. But soldiers aren't.
>
> *A moment, perhaps they listen.*

BOY:

> I could get medicine.

GERONTION:

> You'd forget, grow distracted. Never deliver. And I don't need medicine.

BOY:

Every day, something else is broken with you. Your back, legs, nose.

A pause.

I'd come back. Build a road.

GERONTION:

A road here? God save us.

BOY:

Do something.

GERONTION:

Do something? You'll go to the City if you survive, and you'll think, I should do something, but you won't, you won't, you'll get distracted, you'll settle for the simple life of animals: mating and babies and what's for dinner and oh, it's garbage night, and you'll think the world is such a hole, what's the point, what's the point, better to settle for doing no harm at least, leaving no trace, the smallest possible footprint, you'll shrink yourself and your light and what's for dinner and oh, it's garbage night and you'll learn the names of flowers and dream of better refrigerators and still some bit, some dripping voice in you will say, I should Do Something, Make Something, Leave Something, but you won't you won't you won't.

BOY:

It's not for sure. You don't know. There are no babies anymore, not like that.

GERONTION:

Then one day you'll be blind like me, you'll be old like me, and still you'll think, I should do something, but instead you'll dream of what they'll say at your funeral. How will they remember me? He was a good man, he hid his light, he shrank himself and lived the life of a good and quiet animal, he took his garbage out and separated his tins and paper to be recycled. You'll do something?

BOY:

What do you know?

GERONTION:

I know what happened to me.

BOY:

What?

GERONTION:

Listen, the world is fucked. I understand how you feel, the strange yearnings, the burden. I felt these things too. That's what it means to be human, you donkey. I can explain them to you. But there is nothing to be done. Except to ... wait, keep the worst at bay.

BOY:

I want more.

GERONTION:

More? More is what brought us to this pass.

❧ ❧ ❧

GERONTION and MARIE alone. Silence, except for the sound of her brushing her hair.

GERONTION:

If you've come about the boy ... he's ... He doesn't—he has nothing to do with ... It is the boy isn't it? I know. He—that smell on his skin. Flowers. I remember.

MARIE:

You brought me hyacinths. At first. Then ... it all went to shit.

GERONTION:

Is this why you've come? To ... judge me all over—

MARIE:

Oh, I was joking. I'm not judging you. I'm not ... anything. That's the trouble with language the way we use it. It always sounds like it's doing something to someone. But I don't want to do anything to you. Whatever you feel, it's got nothing to do with me. It's yours, some unresolved crap of your own.

Pause.

Anyway. I was as much to blame as you.

GERONTION:
Blame!

MARIE:
No, no. Listen, there's no why to my being here. You think
there has to be a reason. You think I want something. No.
There's nothing to want.

GERONTION:
Sophistry. Nonsense.

MARIE:
Be quiet now. That's what you want, isn't it? Quiet. Peace?

I did. I wanted to get as far away as I could. And now look.

She laughs.

GERONTION:
I don't understand. How can you be here?

MARIE:
There's no difference between here and there. Not any more.

MARIE kisses him.

GERONTION:
This is only a dream. I'm dreaming again, after so long. That's
all this is.

Kiss me again.

She does. Strange music faintly.

❧ ❧ ❧

Morning. The BOY is very excited, anxious. The dog barking.

GERONTION:
Such dreams. Tenochtitlan. What streets. What music. You ass!
Why did you wake me?

BOY:
People.

GERONTION:
People? Yes? What? Use sentences, egg.

BOY:
In the night.

GERONTION:
You fail. Leave me to—

BOY:
Outside. People.

A silence. GERONTION understands.

GERONTION:
Soldiers?

BOY:
No.

GERONTION:
Tatterdemalions? Have they seen you? People? Are you sure?
How do you know?

BOY:
I heard them. Seen them.

GERONTION:
How close are they?

BOY:
In the fields.

A pause.

GERONTION:
How many?

BOY:
What do we do?

GERONTION:
Wait for them to decamp. Or to find the house, slit our throats,
and dance with our bones.

BOY:

I'll go look.

GERONTION:

No!

BOY:

Just to look. Creep quiet. Like the rats.

GERONTION:

They'll see you. Hear you.

BOY:

No, I'll be quiet.

GERONTION:

No. I forbid it. Stay here. Don't be a fool. They'll find you.
You don't know what they are or what they want.

BOY:

I'll find out.

GERONTION:

No. You will stay here. Bring me my tea.

BOY:

I'll come back fast.

GERONTION:

No no and no. I need you here. Fetch me a blanket. Stay.
We'll play chess.

BOY:

You'll be fine for a little.

GERONTION:

NO.

BOY:

Stop me then.

He goes. GERONTION gasps.

⊷ ⊷ ⊷

GERONTION standing in the room, straining to hear. Outside, the muffled voices of the BOY and the TATTERDEMALION WOMAN. Some laughter. A conversation. The BOY enters with the TATTERDEMALION WOMAN.

BOY:

Welcome to Rat's Alley.

The BOY and the WOMAN have sex. Light slowly up on GERONTION a little way off.

TATTERDEMALION WOMAN:

It's close now. We're close. Already the air is changing, sweeter with the promise. We've finally figured out the exact date. Others tried. Of little faith. And less math. Yes. There. A little …

The WOMAN adjusts the BOY's body slightly.

Uhhuh.

The book says from the first seeds for the first grapes. Right? In other words, from the date when slower. There. From when the seeds were buried. They used to plant in what they called Spring. They used a different calendar from us. Umm. A different calendar. That was the yes now harder mistake with all the others who tried. Yes. But once you know what the date is in our uh huh calendar you just add because it says forty were the days of the swelling waters. From the first seeds for the first grapes. So Uhm. We just count forty days. Fuck. Yes. Forty days from the date of the planting. And we're close now, we can taste it. Up the hard high road along the cold sea and mmmm mmmm they'll be waiting there for us. With songs and sweet wine. And our new bodies. Ready to yes yes yes yes to join the yes Heart of the yeeeees LIGHT. Mmmm. Yes. That will be so sweet.

Thanks. That was good. I should go.

She rearranges her clothes.

BOY:

No. There's … New Bodies. The Silence and the Light. I remember this. A story we were told?

TATTERDEMALION WOMAN:

You could come with us. It doesn't matter if you're not scarred in the right places. It only matters if your intention is pure. They will recognize us by the purity of our intention, not the scars on our skin. That's what we believe.

BOY:

No. Fire fell from the sky.

TATTERDEMALION WOMAN:

I should go though.

↭ ↭ ↭

GERONTION:

Bring me a rug. I'm cold.

BOY:

No more rugs.

Pause.

GERONTION:

. The pain is creeping into my back. Because of the cold today. I suppose. It's worse.

Pause.

Have those seeds come up?

BOY:

No.

GERONTION:

Are you sure?

No answer.

You checked on them? Prayed for them? Nothing come up yet?

BOY:

Nothing comes.

A pause.

GERONTION:

Please don't yell.

A pause.

My back hurts.

A pause.

BOY:

They're gone.

GERONTION:

Hmmm? Gone?

BOY:

They left. Gone.

GERONTION:

Oh yes, the ... Have they?

BOY:

Left. Just muddy tracks inna dirt. Some bones and shit.

GERONTION:

Yes ...

A moment.

We should have had them in. Had them over. To tea. For gammon. And port. We really should have. Too bad. We could have played the Debussey. Next time. Eh? We'll have them over next time.

BOY:

Next ... ?

GERONTION:

Yes, I'm sure they'll be through this way again some time soon and—

BOY:

Nobody comes here. This is dead land, cactus land.

He is upset.

GERONTION:

All right. It's all right. I know, I know, you … liked them. I know. They came. Maybe there'll be another accident?

BOY:

She said something.

GERONTION:

What?

No answer.

Look, what about a game of chess? Bring us the board and we'll play a game, take yer mind off.

BOY:

Heart of the Light.

GERONTION:

What? Heart of what?

BOY:

They're going to the Heart of the Light. For New Bodies.

GERONTION:

Ah. Pilgrims then. Wending their way. The holy blisful martir for to seke.[6] Bearing the knuckle bone of Joseph of Arimathea, no doubt. The Heart of the Light they call it now, do they?

BOY:

The Heart of the Light. The sweet silence. New Bodies. I remember all that. How?

A moment.

Tell me again. How I came to you.

GERONTION:

Play. Bring me a rug. Bring my medicine.

---

6. Chaucer, Prologue to *The Canterbury Tales*.

BOY:

I know about the Heart of the Light, the New Bodies—

GERONTION:

From the television, the squawk box, you confuse your life
with others. You—

BOY:

No. I don't confuse nothing. I remember. Remember. Crowds
of people walking round in a ring.

Jets approach.

Up bridge and down. I see us stumbling over cracked earth.
Who? Who walks always beside me?

*Jets roar overhead. The BOY flinches but does not throw himself to
the ground.*

A sudden chorus of voices, ferocious, and the BOY shouting:

The eye is aflame. Consciousness at the Eye is aflame. The
Tongue is aflame. The Ear is aflame. The Nose is aflame. The
Hand is aflame. Contact at the Hand is aflame. The Senses are
aflame. Consciousness is aflame. Burning.[7]

The chorus fades.

The world is aflame. I remember! We were on our way. To the
Silence. The Heart of the Light. Just like she said! Explain me
this! And we were burning but not like the song, not like the
story. Burning and only burning, not the flame that purifies.
And the planes laughing oversky. Burning. And us falling as
we run.

GERONTION:

You lost your way. It happens. The world is a dangerous place.
More so now than ever. But that is … well, that is … past.

BOY:

No. It's now. It keeps happening. She—

---

7. cf. Buddha's Fire Sermon.

GERONTION:

May be dead by now. Or not. Or safe. There is no way of knowing.

BOY:

There is.

GERONTION:

Don't be a fool, fool. You won't last a—What are you thinking in that dark and dirty brain? What futile dreams, what perfidious hopes are you nursing? You are going to save someone? Do Something? Help? Don't be a fool. You will stay here. With me. I—I—I found you. You would be dead if not for me and so you are bound to me. You can stay here. You can help me. I keep you and claim you. I know you. I recognize you. I see you. I make you. I ... you.

A silence.

The BOY exits.

✧ ✧ ✧

MARIE in a hospital gown.

MARIE:

I dream sometimes—not dreams, they're fantasies. A doctor once asked me if I fantasized about death, and I thought she was either very astute to put it that way, or probably she felt the same way herself.

YOUNG GERONTION:

Which doctor?

MARIE:

Just a doctor. When I was younger.

A silence.

I still have them.

YOUNG GERONTION:

The dreams.

135

MARIE:

Fantasies. I can go quite far into the feeling, into imagining it. I imagine something out of a book. Or maybe more a movie. I probably saw it in a movie. Even my fantasies aren't originals.

YOUNG GERONTION:

Movies have ruined us. Overrun our—

MARIE:

I'm in a long dress, a heavy dress, thick. Falling off a boat, in slow motion in my heavy dress, until I hit the water and I panic, and it all speeds up, and the boat is all of a sudden very far away. I'm screaming but the noise of the boat is so loud of course no one will ever hear me, and the ocean is grey, it's the ocean not a river or, it's grey and cold, nowhere.

YOUNG GERONTION:

… I wish you wouldn't …

MARIE:

I'm trying to tell you something. I'm trying to talk to you.

YOUNG GERONTION:

It's morbid.

MARIE:

Who's morbid?

YOUNG GERONTION:

We can choose. To give in or to put these things—

MARIE:

It's not as simple as all that. You think you just say, I'll put it behind me, I'll move on. People don't move on. We're still living in caves. The brain doesn't work like that. You don't know the first thing about brain and mind. The sense of self, the sense that you order, control, give instructions, is an illusion. You're a goddamn romantic.

Silence.

I was trying to tell you something.

YOUNG GERONTION:

I don't think about death. Rarely think about it. I … think about … I'm not sure what I think about anymore. I used to …. I think about you, about … us. I think about sex.

MARIE:

That's not really thinking though is it?

YOUNG GERONTION:

No, not in the strict sense of … It's more / of a fantasy.

MARIE:

/ Fantasy. Exactly.

They are smiling, amused. Silence.

The water, I don't notice at first how cold it is, and the dress gets heavier and heavier, and eventually, in my fantasy, I give in, I give in to the weight of the dress and let myself be pulled down. But it's a very gentle … pull. I slip under … slowly, like falling asleep. And where it was noisy and desperate and grey above the water, below it's quiet. Quiet. And blue, and the sun is a warm light just overhead that makes everything glow. My arms, my hair, my legs glow. I sink into the blue, farther into the quiet. I can't hear my heart or my breath, it's so quiet and relaxing and all the way into the silence I glow and glow.

YOUNG GERONTION gets up slowly. Goes to her and kisses her on the head.

YOUNG GERONTION:

You should see the garden. The lilacs. You can come home soon. If you want to. It's up to you, they said. I'm there, waiting for you.

He goes, and on his way out shakes hands with GERONTION. MARIE leaves too. GERONTION staggers after them.

GERONTION:

You …

❧ ❧ ❧

GERONTION crawls towards the audience. With difficulty and in pain. He whispers.

GERONTION:

… you …

A little closer.

That corpse you planted … last year in your garden … Has it begun to sprout? Will it bloom this year?

He is almost on the audience when the BOY arrives and gently takes him by the arm back to his chair.

❧ ❧ ❧

GERONTION:

And we used to dance. We'd go dancing, before I was called up.

And walk home after. Our clothes clinging to our skin. The sweat. And sometimes we'd stop, there in the alley, against the garden wall. She would hike up her dress.

Other figures appear and begin to dig, searching for something. Murmur of voices, foreign tongues.

In the warm air and her hair wet stuck against her neck, and sometimes the scent of lilacs or hyacinths. And we'd push there against one another, grind, as if to prove a point. And sometimes the moon—as white and shining as my ass in the streetlight—would fall on her neck, her face. I could see the shape of her head so clearly. Good bones. She was tall. Hah. I stood on my tiptoes. It was never comfortable.

What were we … what did we think we ….

I feel, still feel her breasts like warm birds in my hands.

Ridiculous.

What is the point of this memory now? This fever. What happened? You, child. Why do I tell you these things? Have I embarrassed you?

BOY:

These ghosts. Are they mine or yours?

↭ ↭ ↭

The BOY comes and goes. He brings clothes and other things he
stuffs into a bag.

MARIE appears. She brushes her hair. The noise of her brushing
grows loud. The wind blows hard.

BOY:

I want more. There's more.

GERONTION:

More got us into this mess.

BOY:

It's too late.

GERONTION:

Stay. I'll tell you. The story. Your story. I'll tell it you.

BOY:

I know it.

GERONTION:

I was watching the sky. I watched the planes. I flew you know.
I flew too. And I used to watch. Remembering what it was
like. The spectacle of it.

BOY:

That's not the story.

GERONTION:

I watched for planes, in the fields, when I could still walk that
far … and from there, once, one day I saw the caravan, just a
thin swirl of dust and song. This was you.

BOY:

Me?

GERONTION:

> Your ... people.

> They stopped in the far field. I could just make out the pennon, there, flapping. The sign of the tiger floating above the camp.

BOY:

> Comes the tiger? Sweet tiger. Carry us home.

GERONTION:

> Your fires across the dark and ruined river. Flames, smoke, and song. I watched from afar.

> *The BOY remembers now with clarity.*

BOY:

> Comes the Tiger
> Her claws are quick
> Her teeth they flash
> She chews our skin
> She grinds our bones
> O Sweet Tiger
> Carry us home
> Carry us home ...

GERONTION:

> Another end-time song and dance.

> Planes came. The jets.

> By the time they heard, your people I mean, it was too late. The running and shouting, gathering the few horses. And nowhere to shelter between the rocks and the dried grasses. It was pitiless. Terrible. It's different from the ground. Never saw it like that before. I'd always been in the air. I went out to look, later. And found you. And your sister.

BOY:

> Sister?

GERONTION:

> Perhaps. Burned. Badly.

BOY:
Is this true? Is this the story?

GERONTION:
Never saw it like that. From the air it's different. I picked you up, both of you and carried you. I cut the clothes off your body. They were burned onto you. I washed you in what water there was. I crushed biscuits in tea and fed you both with a dropper. Like birds.

For days I watched and waited. I didn't sleep with wiping your faces and feeding and washing you. That's when I first forgot my drops.

Your sister. She had dark hair and I brushed it. I found one of Marie's brushes and—I told her, I promised to wash her hair, promised her hats and ribbons if she would come back, if she would stay. But she didn't.

You got stronger. Every day till you finally woke up—

BOY:
You said, you were frightened. I scared you.

GERONTION:
I was. You did.

BOY:
You said I was wet, nearly drowned.

GERONTION:
You were nearly dead.

BOY:
Sister?

GERONTION:
She looked something like you.

BOY:
Where ... is she?

GERONTION:
I buried her. In the fields.

BOY:

Outside.

GERONTION:

Not deep enough. Dogs came. Dug her up.

BOY:

You said ... you never said.

GERONTION:

You remembered nothing and I thought ... I thought perhaps you, you were meant to find me. Or I you. (*Pause.*) Meant to care for you. A duty of a kind.

Silence.

BOY:

That's not the story. Is it?

✿ ✿ ✿

The BOY continues packing things: a knife, a hat, gloves.

GERONTION:

Keep the harmonica then. Don't think of me if you play it though. I want to be entirely forgotten. Erased completely. I want to sleep perfectly.

BOY:

Open your arms. Fingers on your left hand. Wiggle them. Keep them up. Fingers on your right. All of life?

He walks into GERONTION's open arms and hugs him. He lifts him up. They waltz. The BOY goes.

GERONTION:

The shops are closing. Quick arms pull windows, draw shutters tight. The lights come on. Another Friday. Or Tuesday. Another 17th of April or 3rd of November. I suppose there are stars.

❦ ❦ ❦

A burial. A line of people. The DIGGER digging. A priest speaks.
Some humming. The mourners wait and wait, expecting
something to happen, something to grow on or from the grave.
One eventually looks to the sky. One turns away. The priest
lights a cigarette. Another puts her head to the fresh earth on the
grave, listening. One at a time they eventually wander away,
disappointed, crying. Finally, only one is left with the DIGGER
who continues to cover the body. The LAST MAN (YOUNG
GERONTION) pulls out a handphone. He dials, waits, and
wanders the grounds. We can only hear some of what he says.

LAST MAN:
 I'm here ... No, nothing ... We did everything as—
Scrupulously. I was ... I am. Right now ... No, everyone's
gone. Abandoned all hope ... I said everyone has left already
... It's been some time. I don't know ... quite a while. I don't
really know. Forever perhaps ... Oh ...

He sees the DIGGER, waiting.

Just a ... a moment ...

He pays the DIGGER. The DIGGER tips his cap, goes.

Thank you. (*on phone again*) No, had to pay the, the ... digger.
So ...

He takes another look at the gravesite, still hoping something
might happen.

No. It's not ... I'm on my way then ...

He exits.

❦ ❦ ❦

GERONTION surrounded by figures digging steadily. MARIE is
there, brushing her hair. A dog barks. Gathering dark. The rumble

143

of thunder. A flash of lightning and illuminated in the flash, the BOY suddenly appears, wet and frightened. The sound of rain. GERONTION speaks with the thunder. Lightning. The BOY stands unmoving. Rain falls. Darkness. Rain and thunder.

THE END